Support for *In*

"Sunny Dawn Johnston's in-person radiance and charisma come through the printed page, as well. The simple yet effective techniques she shares to connect with the angelic realm are an important addition to the field and will be of help to those on the path."

—Steven Halpern, bestselling author of *Chakra Suite*,
composer/recording artist/sound healer

"At times, we all need a guide who can skillfully escort us through challenges. In this inspirational book, Sunny Dawn Johnston is such a guide. *Invoking the Archangels* will teach you how to connect with the Angels, help you heal, and inspire you toward a greater life."

—Laura Alden Kamm, author of *Intuitive Wellness:*
Using Your Body's Inner Wisdom to Heal

"Sunny Dawn Johnston is authentic and powerful in her ability to teach us how to connect with the angelic realm. If you want to develop a relationship with the Archangels to assist you in your own personal healing, read *Invoking the Archangels: A Nine-Step Process to Heal Your Body, Mind, and Soul.*"

—Peggy Rometo, intuitive healer/psychic/medium
and author of *The Little Book of Big Promises*

"Bravo to Sunny Dawn Johnston for writing such a courageous and brave book about healing the heart. Her story is very compelling, and it clearly illustrates the powerful and loving energy of the Archangels. Through her words, Sunny creates a safe haven for readers to explore and heal such intimate areas as relationships, finances, addictions, and health. This book is a winner, and I highly recommend it."

—Bronwyn Marmo, bestselling and award-winning author
of *The Food Is a Lie: The Truth Is Within*

"Miracles are not only possible, they are necessary—if we are to fulfill our true purpose. Sunny Dawn Johnston is a living testament to that reality. As we each make our pilgrimage from living a body-centered intellectual life to a soul-centered intuitive one, Sunny's step-by-step guide to invoking the healing wisdom and power of the Archangels comes as a gift from heaven. Whether you are looking for a ray of hope and inspiration in these challenging times, or you are ready to transform your whole life, pick up a copy of this book before you take another step. Learn from someone who's been there and returned to show us how."

—Michael J. Tamura, spiritual teacher, clairvoyant education and healing pioneer, and award-winning author of *You Are the Answer*

"In her classic work, *Invoking the Archangels: A Nine-Step Process to Heal Your Body, Mind, and Soul*, Sunny Dawn Johnston makes the wisdom, love, and healing of the Archangels accessible to everyone. Whether you have intuitive talent or not, you can use her nine-step process to connect with the loving beings that are ready to help you with every facet of your life. This is a 'must have' addition to any collection of Angel books and a great read if you are just starting to explore your relationship with your heavenly helpers."

—Ann Albers, author, lecturer, and Angel communicator

"Sunny's work is simply awesome!! I have experienced her message firsthand and had a profound opening in my own heart that has deepened my connection to my Self and allowed me to breathe in the joy of being with the angelic realm. I love this work!"

—Shawn Gallaway, singer/songwriter, author, visual artist, and healer

"The touching, moving, and inspiring 'never giving up hope even when the going gets tough' life story of Sunny Dawn Johnston will make even the nonbelievers believe . . . in the power of the Archangels."

—Shayne Traviss, founder of VividLife.me

"Sunny beautifully radiates authenticity and courage! This fascinating book offers a fresh perspective on leading an openhearted life of love and self-discovery. Truth, insight, and words of wisdom for those looking to heal the heart!"

Lisa McCourt, Hay House author of
Juicy Joy—7 Simple Steps to Your Glorious, Gutsy Self

"Sunny shines again. *Invoking the Archangels* is a personal story of transformation with lessons for us all. Sunny's conversational method of teaching in person moves effortlessly to this book. I can hear her voice and see her speaking every word on these written pages. Every reader will experience personal spiritual growth with the easy-to-follow exercises, which come at just the right moments. Sunny's charisma and warmth radiate. Her insights will change you."

—Scott Davis, producer/writer

"Sunny writes the way she lives, with inspirational thoughts and clarity of purpose. She's an honest storyteller and a delight to be with, both in person and on the page. You will find this book full of new approaches to living, all delivered with enthusiasm by a person who deserves the name Sunny Dawn."

—Paul Perry, *New York Times* bestselling author

"In *Invoking the Archangels*, Sunny Dawn Johnston shares a magical recipe of angelic knowledge, heart-centered exercises, and life experiences that nourish the soul's purpose and passions!"

—Barry Goldstein, Grammy Award–winning producer

Invoking the Archangels is an amazing book written by a powerful teacher—Sunny Dawn Johnston! You will gain much clarity and understanding about the roles that Angels play in our lives, and you will not be able to put this book down. Sunny explains things in a way that makes perfect sense, and she will guide you into a place of deep healing. It is a must read!

Liz Dawn Donahue, CEO & co-founder of
Mishka Productions and the Celebrate Your Life conference

SUNNY DAWN JOHNSTON

INVOKING THE ARCHANGELS

A NINE-STEP PROCESS TO HEAL YOUR BODY, MIND, AND SOUL

Hierophant publishing

Cover design by Adrian Morgan
Interior and cover author photos by Lynn Korf
Text layout by Jane Hagaman

Hierophant Publishing
www.hierophantpublishing.com

If you are unable to order this book from your local
bookseller, you may order directly from the publisher.

Library of Congress Control Number: 2011936072

ISBN 978-0-9818771-4-3
10 9 8 7 6 5 4 3 2

Printed on acid-free paper in the United States

This book is dedicated to
all of my teachers . . .
both physical and nonphysical

Namasté

Contents

SECTION 4 / PAGE 69
HEALING YOUR HEART:
A Nine-Step Archangel Process

SECTION 5 / PAGE 107
WORKING WITH THE
NINE-STEP ARCHANGEL PROCESS

SECTION 6 / PAGE 149
GUIDED ANGEL MEDITATIONS

SECTION 7 / PAGE 155
A FEW CLIENTS' ANGELIC EXPERIENCES

APPENDIX / 165

SUGGESTED READING / 173

Appreciation

My appreciation begins with Spirit. I am grateful for the experiences I've had. Each one has allowed me to grow, and I am blessed to live the spiritual life I live. I am honored that Spirit entrusts me with the knowledge and wisdom that I've gained along my own personal journey and that I continue to discover each day I live my life.

I have been blessed with the support of many wonderful beings, both physical and nonphysical. Many people have touched my life and made an impression on my soul. There are only so many ways to say thank you, and without knowing several languages, my gratitude will likely be repetitive. Trying to express the appreciation I have in my heart toward everyone who has supported this book would take more pages than the finished product. With that being said, I'll begin.

To my mom, Solara: You started this journey for me many years ago. I am eternally grateful to you for being that guide for me. You had the knowing and courage to begin a new spiritual journey yourself and by opening that door you introduced me to the wonderful world of the unseen. Through you, I have learned compassion, understanding, and empathy. Thank you for being a patient, loyal, and compassionate teacher to me. You are one of the most beautiful people I know. I will always see you as the magnificent light that you are. Despite the hardships you have endured, you remain a loving force in a sometimes difficult world. I love you! Love, your daughter of *Light!*

To my husband, Brett: You are the love of my life and my best friend. I know that we attracted this relationship into creation that special evening eighteen years ago. I am forever blessed to have my dreams of a wonderful, supportive husband answered. You have been my rock, grounding energy, voice of reason, and support through many twists and turns, ups and downs, and amazing experiences. Through each and every one of them, you've loved me unconditionally and have inspired me to be a better woman every day. You challenge me to love our differences unconditionally, and I am so appreciative of your willingness to do the same. Your love is my greatest blessing.

To my son Crew: I thank you for being who you are and for being patient with me as I have become who I am. You have been my greatest teacher, and I am healthier and happier because of you. Thank you for loving me through the eyes of a child and being such an incredible young man. You amaze me every day, while inspiring others, and I am so proud to be your mom. I love you forever!

To my son Arizona: You are my light! You are a gift from Spirit. Your sweet smile, sense of humor, and sparkling eyes continue to be a source of love and inspiration for me. Your spirit lifts me up, and your voice puts a smile in my heart. You are an amazing child and have taught me to lighten up and have fun! I love you to infinity and beyond!

To my dad: You taught me strength and wisdom and to never say the word "can't." I rarely do. You taught me to be strong in the face of adversity, to get back up when I've fallen down, and how to live fully in each moment. You taught me some of my greatest lessons about love, acceptance, integrity, and tolerance, and I will always be grateful to you for that. I love you.

To my brother Andrew: We have grown up together, and I thank you for supporting me through emotionally and physically tough times. You gave me the "time outs" I needed when I was a single parent and kept me from going crazy by providing peace and quiet. I so appreciate it. Ever since the day I met you, I knew you were my brother, because our hearts immediately connected. I love you.

To my little brother Shad: There is always someone in the family who makes you laugh out loud. I appreciate your humor and impersonations. You make me laugh anytime and at anything. You are a comedian at heart, and your humor reminds me to laugh out loud more often. I appreciate the energy and excitement you have for life. You radiate fun and laughter. You remind me to take a time out, to stop and play, and I *love* that about you! I love you.

To my students and clients: I stand in appreciation of each and every one of you! You teach me to be present, loving, and mindful. Each one of you inspires me to be a better person, to show up for myself, to live life full out, and to continue moving forward. Thank you for teaching me, day by day, to honor myself. Thank you to the many volunteers who have supported my healing center, Sunlight Alliance LLC. It would not be what it is today without your love, support, and participation.

I am blessed to have had many supportive people on my journey. To name them all would take a book itself.

THANK YOU, LIZ, JAIME, AND ARIEL: Many years ago I was an unknown, and you saw something in me and gave me a chance. You opened a door, and I am forever grateful for the opportunities that have manifested since then. Thank you for listening to your hearts.

TO MY PUBLISHER, RANDY DAVILA: I thank you for the incredible opportunity you have given me to share my experiences in this book. It has been a lifelong dream, and fear, that I can now say I have obtained, and overcome. Yay!

AND FINALLY, TO MY SUNLIGHT TEAM, AMY, DEB, KRIS, AND ROBIN: There is no way to thank you ladies for everything you have done to support me, my work, the healing center, and my vision. I am blessed to have you all as friends, but truly honored to call you family. Thank you for helping me take baby steps to give up control of almost every aspect of my business, so I could be of better service to others by writing this book. Thank you for being patient as I changed my mind from moment to moment. Thank you for helping me to see that I didn't need to do it all and, most importantly, for holding my hand on the days when I wasn't sure if I could. Those are the days I am the most grateful for the support of each one of you. I love you all, unconditionally.

There are still so many more people I want to acknowledge and I know that *you* know who you are. From the very beginning, I have had people step in and out of my life to help me along the way. I hope that as you read this, you truly do know who *you* are, and take a breath with me as I share with you the greatest prayer I know . . .

Thank you!

Namasté,
Sunny Dawn Johnston

Introduction

My name is Sunny Dawn, and, yes, "Sunny Dawn" is my birth name. That is the first question I am often asked when someone meets me for the first time or hears my name. My birth name is the perfect vibration for me, and my mother knew that when she picked it out when she was fifteen. My mom only had to wait another six years for my grand entrance into the physical world, and, oh boy, was it grand!

The second most common question I am asked is, "Are you Mormon?" I spent ten years of my childhood growing up in Salt Lake City, Utah, and when people hear that, they naturally assume I am Mormon. Well the answer to that question is no, I am not Mormon. My religion is simply *Love!* When I was three years old and living in the Philippines, I witnessed extreme abuse in the name of religion, and that experience changed my perception of religion forever. I would say that I am "spiritual" rather than religious, as spirituality more closely aligns with my vibration.

At age thirteen, I had my first angelic experience; I saw my first Angel. I was surprised when I awoke to a brilliant, glowing, angelic being hovering above my bed. But I wasn't afraid, because the peaceful energy that emanated from this glow felt like pure love. I soaked it up and felt calm, serene, and supported as I drifted back to sleep.

This was my first experience with the angelic realm, and I continued to have many more throughout my life. Even though each experience was different, the energy of absolute unconditional love was the same. Regardless of what was going on in my life, the angelic realm was always present. Sometimes I chose to listen, other times not. I denied, resisted, and even ignored them, yet they still remained. This is the unconditional love that is available to each and every one of you, every moment of your life.

The last twenty-six years have been an amazing journey, and each day I've experienced divine intervention in the form of Angels, Archangels, Spirit Guides, Ascended Masters, and the beautiful physical bodies that walk this planet with me. I've learned that I am responsible for my life. I created my challenges by my own resistance to love. I was born with innate value, simply because I was born into a physical body. I did not need to earn, prove, or justify my worth. I was worthy because I was. I forgot that simple statement many times in my life. Perhaps you have also. There was no one to blame and nothing at fault. It was part of my path, a very important part of my path—maybe the most important! The pain, discomfort, challenge, or lack were all awarenesses that led to my acknowledgment of my own self-worth. The Archangels surrounded me and guided me while I was given opportunities to see my unique and divine value. The choice was mine, as it is yours.

The stories that I share with you on the following pages are my experiences of worthiness, lack, abundance, and everything in between. That being said, I want to assure you that the stories in this book are true, based on my experience and perception. Hidden between the words and phrases is the simple truth that we are always unconditionally loved by the angelic realm and that everything happens for a reason, even when the reason isn't clear at the time.

Over the past decade, I have worked with thousands of clients as a spiritual counselor and psychic medium, taught hundreds of classes on Communicating with Your Angels, Psychic Development and Mediumship, and through them all, continue to witness different experiences with the Archangels. Some clients talk to them, others feel them, some see them, and a few can even hear their messages; however, a large majority are not aware of them consciously, even though they believe in them. So they come to me and ask me to share what their Angels are saying. My mission is to change that! Part of the reason that my clients do not feel as if they can communicate with their Angels is because they feel unworthy. I, too, have felt that unworthiness, so I understand.

Based on my experiences, I created a process that uses the energy of the seven Archangels to heal the heart from the inside out. When you can begin to see, feel, and know your true value, your innate worthiness, the healing begins. Once you begin to love yourself, as the Archangels love you, you will want to use this process in every challenging area of your life. This process can also be used for relationships, addictions, career issues, health issues, and more. Through these pages, I will teach you how to invoke the power of the Archangels to help transform your heart from a state of fear to a realization of the love that always exists within. Are you ready? Of course you are. The time is now! Just turn the page and let's begin.

Who Are Our Spiritual Helpers?

Angels can unleash hurricanes of healing,
release tidal waves of love,
move whole mountains of hatred,
melt icebergs of jealousy
and evaporate oceans of pain.

—Unknown

Everything created is energy, and energy vibrates at different levels. Just as a singer has a vocal range that moves from lowest to highest, so do human beings have a vibrational range. In other words, you move up and down a vibrational scale. The more you work on loving yourself, the higher your vibration rises and the easier it is to connect with the higher vibrational beings that I refer to as Spiritual Helpers. These helpers are also known as deceased loved ones, Spirit Guides, Ascended Masters, Angels, and Archangels. Everyone is born with a different vibrational scale, but everyone possesses the ability to reach the highest level through appreciation, forgiveness, joy, meditation, and love. If you wish to connect to higher vibrational beings, then you simply raise your own personal vibration.

You might be wondering why *you* need to raise *your* vibration. The universal Law of Attraction states that like energy attracts like energy; and because the beings in the spiritual realm will not lower their vibration, you must raise yours to connect with them. The more you stay in a higher, lighter, clearer vibration, the more you will connect with the spiritual realm. I have included a diagram of the energetic vibrational scale below. This will give you an idea of the vibrational ranges of Spiritual Helpers as I have come to experience and understand them. Each level is not good or bad, it just simply is. I have defined the energy of each vibration in my own terms, so you can better understand my chart.

Physical beings are you and me and everyone you see with a body and a heartbeat.

Deceased loved ones are family, friends, co-workers, and loved ones who have passed away, transitioned, kicked the bucket, died, dropped their body, and so on. They have released the dense energy of their physical bodies and have automatically moved up the vibrational scale. Deceased loved ones can raise their vibration even higher now and can become Spirit Guides, if so desired and chosen. In my experience, there is often an amount of divine time, not measured time, where they "prepare" for this, as it is not typically instantaneous.

Spirit Guides, who once inhabited a physical form, had the same journey or purpose as the physical beings they are

Energetic Vibrational Scale

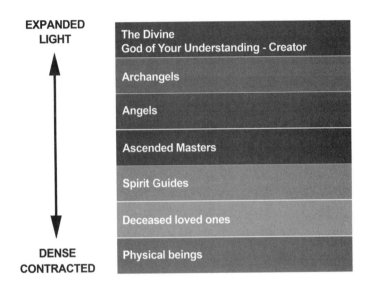

EXPANDED
LIGHT

The Divine
God of Your Understanding - Creator

Archangels

Angels

Ascended Masters

Spirit Guides

Deceased loved ones

DENSE
CONTRACTED

Physical beings

now guiding. Upon leaving their physical bodies, Spirit Guides choose to become teachers or guides to those of us still in the physical realm. They offer guidance, comfort, and, at times, warnings and protection. Spirit Guides are often the spiritual essence of deceased loved ones.

The Ascended Masters are Divine Beings that lived earthly lives as great teachers, healers, or way-showers of ascension. They released all their fears and grew and raised their vibrations in order to ascend. Ascended Masters come from all cultures, modern and ancient civilizations, and are often spoken of and remembered in religious context, such as Buddha and Jesus. The Ascended Masters bring light and love to everyone regardless of their religious beliefs or feelings of worthiness. The Ascended Masters know and teach that we are all worthy of love and guidance.

Angels, Guardian Angels, and Archangels are higher vibrational beings who exist only in the spiritual realm and do not incarnate into physical form as humans and animals do. **Angels** help, guide, comfort, and assist us in our earthly journey by uplifting and protecting us. Each physical being is supported by one **Guardian Angel** throughout his/her entire physical life, from birth to death. A Guardian Angel's job is to unconditionally love and protect us. **Archangels** are the powerful overseers of the angelic realm. Call on the Archangels any time for anything, and they will be there immediately.

Throughout my life, angelic beings have presented themselves in all sorts of shapes, sizes, and forms. Their appearance was often determined by what I was feeling, seeing, or knowing in the moment. Over time though, their forms have changed and evolved as I've grown spiritually. Therefore, the definition or visual representation of Angels can be as different as seashells on a beach. Each individual will experience Angels based upon his or her own perceptions. I believe that all impressions of the angelic realm are valid. Angels show themselves in a way that you are able to perceive and understand and are often gentle and comforting in their approach.

The Divine is the God of your understanding. My understanding of God does not come from religious beliefs or scripture but from my own journey inward. When I reached a point in my life where I recognized I had to take responsibility for myself and that I had no control over anything or anyone but myself, I came to understand that God was in everyone and everything. I realized that God is *Love*. I am God, you are God, we are God. As are the wind, the trees, the ocean, the animals, the clouds, the rainbows, and the sun. The God of my understanding is everywhere, in everything, and is simply Love.

SECTION 2

How Do I Connect
with the Archangels?

Angels transcend every religion, every philosophy, every
creed. In fact angels have no religion as we know it . . .
their existence precedes every religious system that has
ever existed on earth.

—St. Thomas Aquinas

The angelic realm's mission is to protect, nurture, and
guide humanity. Races, cultures, and religions may have
diverse and conflicting doctrines, but they all have one thing
in common—a belief in Angels. In fact, 85 percent of all
religions reference Angels in some form or another.

Angelic beings team up to assist us in connecting the
physical world to the spiritual world. Angels offer unconditional love, which is the essence of all that is. Open yourself
up to the possibility that Angels exist and invite them to
help you with self-love, well-being, abundance, love, pros-
perity, peace, and joy. By asking, you allow them to assist on
your behalf. Angels always honor free will and act only once
invited, so remember to ask.

A Four-Step Process

There is a simple four-step process that will assist you in connecting with the Archangels.

1. **Ask**—Begin by asking for assistance: For the angels to help in any area of your life, you must first "ask" for their assistance. There is no right or wrong way to do this. A simple intention works just as well as a verbal expression or a telepathic conversation. Simply saying, "Angels, please help me," is enough. Asking in a way that feels appropriate to you will ensure that the Angels will answer your call and stand by your side. The important step is to recognize that you are in need of support, guidance, direction, encouragement, etc., and be willing to ask for it.

2. **Allow**—Release the need to control the situation and be open to receive: Allowing is as easy as "getting out of your own way." When you release the need to control situations, people, and emotions and just allow the flow and the laws of the Universe to work on your behalf, then you open up room for all of the good to come into your life. Allowing frees up your energy to do the things that make you happy and to receive the abundance that is innately yours. Your Angels always see your life from the perspective of allowing. They support that vision "for you" and "within you" until you are able to feel it for yourself. The sooner you learn to let go of resistance and start affirming what you desire, the sooner you will come into alignment with what

you are asking for. Once the asking and allowing are in alignment with one another, then you are well on your way to believing.

3. **Believe**—Trust that the Angels will guide you in perfect divine time: Trust can be one of the most difficult attitudes to adopt, especially when you do not have any evidence that you will receive what you desire. Trusting typically requires you to be vulnerable with others and, in this case, with the Angels. I made a decision a long time ago when I started working with the angelic realm, and that decision was to give up "suspicions." I made a conscious choice to be optimistic rather than pessimistic, and that choice proved to be instrumental in my working relationship with my Archangels. So it is your choice to trust that you are being guided in the perfect divine time. If you are feeling a desire from your heart, trust that the Angels will guide you in the perfect way for your highest good.

4. **Receive**—Listen to your intuitive guidance and give thanks: You've asked, allowed, and believed. The last step is to now receive. Your Archangels and guides will send you many messages. It could be a song on the radio, the flicker of a light, a sign on a bus, the letters on a license plate. Messages come in many ways and many forms, and I ask that you be open to receiving them in ways that may be new or different to you. As the messages and signs appear, you will find that they will validate that you are on the right path. And, finally, remember to give thanks for the abundance, joy, happiness,

and love that are presently in your life. Don't give up five minutes before the miracle happens. Stay open to receive all that is yours.

Developing Your Personal Relationship with Each Archangel

In my experience, this process has allowed me to connect to the energy of each Archangel and to allow healing to occur on many levels. It is important to me that you have your own experience with each Archangel, so I have created an exercise to assist you in developing that relationship. I recommend you do this *first*, before you read anything further about the Archangels or learn any more than you already know. This is an experiential exercise based on *your* intuitive guidance. You will need to complete the worksheet here, or you can go to the interactive website www.invoking thearchangels.com to download a copy. The worksheet lists each day of the week in a column down the left hand side. I'd like you to write down one of the following colors next to each day of the week: blue, pink, yellow, green, white, red, and violet. Let your intuition guide you and ask your Angels for assistance. Once you have matched one of the seven colors to one of the days of the week, turn to page 12 and continue reading. I will explain how to use this exercise next. Trust me and have fun!

(Blue, Pink, Yellow, Green, White, Red, and Violet)

Monday ___blue___

Tuesday ___pink___

Wednesday ___green___

Thursday ___violet___

Friday ___red___

Saturday ___yellow___

Sunday ___white___

Okay, did you do it? Don't read any further if you have not done the exercise. Stop, do the exercise, and then come back. You cannot get this one wrong, I promise.

When you have completed the exercise, you will have assigned yourself a particular color for each day of the week. Note that each color vibrates to a particular Archangel. (See section 3 for the Archangel color vibrations.) What I want you to do is invoke an Archangel each day of the week and work with his energy and color for that day. For example, if you chose yellow for Monday and green for Tuesday, you would invoke Archangel Jophiel on Monday and Archangel Raphael on Tuesday. You will invoke their energy through your thoughts and intention, but I'd like you to go a step further and find something physical to represent them. This could be a specific stone or a piece of clothing that is the same color as the Archangel you are working with. Since we are physical beings, sometimes it is beneficial to have a physical connection to help attract each Archangel's energy to you.

I encourage you to visualize their energy surrounding you, and to ask them to show you a sign. Talk with the Archangel throughout the day, and begin to develop your own personal relationship. When the day is complete, journal your experience. Write about the big things, the little things, the coincidental, and the unusual. Oftentimes when you walk through your day consciously, you begin to see a pattern of how this Archangel showed up.

This exercise helped me develop my own personal relationship with the Archangels, and it is my hope that it will do the same for you. I encourage you to create your relationship with each Archangel based on *your* experience, rather than someone else's perception.

Introducing the Seven Archangels

> Do not search for us, we will find you.
> Do not wait for us, we are here . . . all ready.
> Do not whisper your name, we know it well.
> We have loved you forever, time will tell . . .
> We are your Guardian Angels.
>
> —Unknown

I would like to introduce the seven Archangels as I have experienced them. You may have had similar or different experiences, and the value of those experiences is that we can learn from all of them. I do not believe in a "right" or "wrong" way to connect with the Angels. I simply believe in the presence and perception of angelic vibrations.

Archangel Michael

Pronounced MY-kuhl, it means "He who is like God." Michael is the Archangel of protection, guidance, and strength.

HELPS WITH: Protection, direction, self-esteem, motivation, courage, commitment, faith, energy, vitality, life's purpose, and releasing fear.

COLOR VIBRATION: Brilliant Blue

GEMSTONE: Lapis Lazuli

INVOCATION: I invoke the blue light of Archangel Michael to surround me and protect me from any negative energy or entities, seen or unseen. I ask that I be a channel of divine love and healing to everyone I cross paths with. I ask for courage, strength, and faith so that I may walk this earth with an open heart and an open mind. Thank you for the true and perfect guidance that surrounds me each and every moment . . . and so it is!

As I invoke Archangel Michael, I visualize a blue bubble—like an energy field around me—and imagine that I can see, hear, feel, and know that his energy of protection surrounds me on all levels.

PERSONAL EXPERIENCE: I was first introduced to the powerful energy of Archangel Michael at the age of thirteen. This experience changed my life forever and connected me to the angelic realm in amazing and incredible ways. It happened in the spring of 1984. My brother Shad, five years old at the time, was born with intuitive gifts, just as I was. His intuitive gift was sight (clairvoyance), and he was able to see the Spirit world. He could see Angels and therefore befriended many of them. I, on the other hand, was clairsentient. I could feel the presence of the Angels, but I could not see them. Angels come in a form that you believe to be true, so my brother saw them as brightly colored triangles, squares, and circles with wings.

Shad played with his "friends," as he referred to them, and they accompanied him wherever he went. Often I'd feel impatient as I waited for them to get into the car. Sometimes I'd close the door of the car just to see what would happen, and Shad would yell at me because they were not all in yet. We'd bicker at the grocery store because we had to wait for his "friends" to get into the shopping cart. Shad talked about how much he loved them and how they were always with him. They just annoyed me and added to the frustrations of my life. My parents were struggling with money, and many arguments could be heard throughout our household. The energy in our home was heavy.

One evening, my parents asked me to baby-sit Shad so that they could go to dinner. This was my first time watching him by myself, and I was up for the challenge. As my brother was hanging out with his "friends," I started to feel this heaviness in my body. It kind of freaked me out. At the same time, Shad began crying because his colorful friends had disappeared, and he now saw friends with scary faces. Tears streamed down his face as he described the wingless black, brown, and green shapes. We were both scared, and I didn't know what to do, so I asked for help. I prayed that we would be okay, and I took my brother's hand and walked to the back of the house. We sat against a brick wall so nothing could get behind us. This happened before cell phones or pagers were around, so our only choice was to wait it out. Four hours passed and finally my parents came home. I was relieved to see them, and I demanded that they do something to make these scary feelings go away. Mom assured me that she would call her psychic friend Leo in the morning and ask her to come over and do a clearing and blessing on the house. Needless to say, that evening my brother and I slept with our parents.

Leo arrived in the morning. As she entered our house, she could see and feel the heaviness. She explained that she would say a prayer of protection and ask the Angels to clear the negative energy. When I heard that, the skeptic in me came out. I had a hard time believing that a prayer and simple request would get them to leave. My prayer had not worked the night before, so why should this one? Since I was living under my parents' roof, I really had no other choice but to give it a try.

I followed Leo and my mother into the foyer of our house. As we walked along the hall, I saw Shad outside riding his Big Wheel up and down the sidewalk. As I watched his playful spirit, Leo explained that she was going to invoke Archangel Michael and ask him to protect the home and release the negative energy. It sounded good, but I did not believe it. We entered the foyer, and Leo asked me and my mom to hold hands with her and each other, stand in a circle, and close our eyes. I kept one eye open because, being a skeptic at heart, I needed some validation. I thought to myself, show me a sign, a flash of light, a sudden drop in temperature, a loud noise, something. Show me "something" that will make me believe that this is all real. My thoughts were interrupted by the strength of Leo's voice.

She said, "I invoke the blue light of Archangel Michael to surround and protect this home from any negative energy or entities, seen or unseen . . . and so it is!" That was it. That was the prayer. I didn't see anything. There was no flash of light, no sudden drop in temperature, no loud noise, nothing. I didn't feel anything except frustration and doubt. My mom, however, experienced chills up and down her body. She exclaimed, "Wow, it already feels so much clearer and lighter in here."

I rolled my eyes and started to walk away. As I entered the living room, Shad came running through the front door. As my eyes met his, I was taken aback by the expression on his face. With both eyes wide open, he excitedly said, "Mommy, there is great big blue bubble around our house!" I looked at him, then my mom, then Leo. In that moment, I had received the validation I was looking for through the eyes of my brother Shad. That moment changed who I would become.

As soon as you intend, invoke, call in, invite, or request the Archangels' presence, they are there! They are there whether you recognize them or not. In my experience, I was so wrapped up in wanting physical proof that I missed the gift of "feeling" Archangel Michael's presence. This experience taught me to stay open to the way in which the Angels' messages come through to me. I promised myself that I would not try to control or dictate the way in which they came. If you are a natural feeler, as I was, and you want to "see" your Angels, you might be disappointed. Accepting your own natural intuitive gifts unlocks the door to all the others. However, if you want an experience that is outside your own natural gifts, then oftentimes the validation and gift are missed. By staying open and receptive, you allow your Angels to communicate with you easily and often.

VALUE OF THE EXPERIENCE: When you invoke the Archangels, they are there immediately, regardless of what your physical senses may observe. Trust that when you ask, it is given, and when you invoke, they are present.

Archangel Jophiel

Pronounced JOE-fee-el, it means "Beauty of God." Jophiel is the Archangel of creativity, beauty, and art.

HELPS WITH: Manifesting more beauty in our lives through our thoughts, supporting artists and artistic projects, interior design and decorating, releasing prejudice and ignorance, awakening, self-awareness, inspiration, hope, and joy. Helps those who feel spiritually lost, depressed, or in despair.

COLOR VIBRATION: Golden Yellow

GEMSTONE: Citrine

INVOCATION: I invoke the golden-yellow light of Archangel Jophiel. Help me to manifest beauty within and around me. Jophiel, I know that I am a creative being, and I ask that you help me to use that creative power in every aspect of my life. Please help me to remember that whatever I focus on is manifested through the vibration of my own thoughts. Help me to align my thoughts with who I really am and to see the beauty in all that crosses my path. Allow me to remain open-minded and be guided by the light within. With your help and creative power, I can and will manifest the beautiful life of my dreams . . . and so it is!

As I invoke Archangel Jophiel, I visualize a golden-yellow light entering the top of my head and moving down my entire body. This vibrating light encases me in a safe and comfortable energy field. I see, hear, feel, and know that the energy of creativity and manifestation surrounds me and dwells within me at all times.

PERSONAL EXPERIENCE: Archangel Jophiel helps you manifest more beauty in your life through your thoughts. His energy helps you manifest your heart's deepest desires and sometimes makes you aware of desires that are buried. If you are working on changing your thought patterns about your own self-worth, body image, or your present-day experiences in the physical world, then call on Jophiel.

Even though I know Archangel Jophiel supported and surrounded me most of my life, I had many experiences where my negative thought patterns created my everyday life. I did not heed his guidance and wisdom for many years, and I chose to stay in states of anger, frustration, fear, and self-criticism. His loving energy never left my side, and as I look back while writing this book, I realize that he was always opening up doors for me to see my true light. Unfortunately, I wasn't willing to walk through those doors for many, many years.

There were many experiences that I had while growing up that led to a lack of self-worth, beginning at a very early age. The first time I remember questioning my worth was at age six. My parents were trying to have another baby, and my mom had already suffered two miscarriages. I remember walking into the bathroom one morning while she was in the process of miscarrying a third time, and I immediately felt responsible for her sadness and pain. As a very young child, I wondered why she would put herself through all of this agony when she had me. I started wondering why I wasn't enough. This was my first conscious memory of questioning my value and worth. As an adult, I know that her desire to have another child had nothing to do with me being good enough, but as a child, I took responsibility for my parents' happiness. My lack of self-esteem weaved its way through almost every area of my life.

Before age eight, I would say I was a pretty typical kid. I got straight As, had friends and a pretty easygoing attitude. I was an only child until that age, so I was used to getting my own way. I had no one to compete and argue with, I was loved a bunch, given everything I wanted, and had it made. I was a happy little girl. My friends would say I was bossy, selfish, and sometimes argumentative, but what spoiled child wasn't?

My parents finally had another child, my younger brother Shad. Within months we were moving to Wyoming for a job transfer my dad had accepted, only to move back to Utah nine months later. This caused extreme amounts of stress and tension in the household. My little brother was quite a handful and sick often, so he took up most of my mom's time. My dad was busy at work, so my mom was on her own with us kids most of the time. I spent many hours alone, which I was used to because I had been an only child, but there were times when it really bothered me. I missed our family time, but what upset me more was the fighting. My mom wanted to be near her family in Utah, and I could feel her anger, pain, and sadness at being forced to move. I never voiced those feelings; it was just an awareness I had of a deep sense of pain, sadness, and, at times, hopelessness that I felt from her. She was a wonderful mom, would do anything for me and my brother, and did. But there always seemed to be an underlying sadness that I could feel; and for reasons unknown to either one of us, I felt responsible for her.

When I was little, I was Daddy's girl. I spent a great deal of time with him. I was his right-hand gal, and I'd go everywhere with him. At the age of nine, I even started working in the family business during the summers. At first I loved it, but over the next seven years, I grew to resent the work, and my dad. When I was about twelve, I noticed that my easygoing attitude started to fade. I felt less accepted in the community as my friends spent more time at church, and I felt left out. I tried fitting in by going to church with them, but every time I tried to make myself go, it felt forced or fake. It didn't feel right for me, so I eventually stopped going. I felt disconnected from my dad, too.

As I became more mature, we connected less, and he started criticizing me more. Deep down inside, I was identifying less with those around me and feeling separate from everyone. There were days when I didn't even feel like I belonged on the planet. My negative thoughts were present for many hours of the day, as I would imagine a place I could go to and just disappear. I began writing sad and sometimes disturbing poems about my life and my perceptions of life.

I became increasingly self-critical, and that internal criticism manifested itself as external judgment. I was judgmental of nearly everything and everyone around me. It was at that time, around age thirteen, that I began to gain weight. This was my way of protecting myself from the feelings and emotions I was carrying within and didn't know how to deal with. I didn't understand at the time that I was a sensitive

child, picking up on the energy of everyone in my environment. Over the next couple of years, I put on about fifty
pounds, and as I got bigger, I questioned my value and self-
worth over and over again. I was depressed, frustrated, sad,
and spiraling out of control. My mom expressed her concern
for me by trying to help in every way she could. My dad just
teased me about it.

My mom did her very best to support me. She tried everything. She took me shopping to buy new clothes in the
hopes that I would "feel" better. However, I left feeling worse
because nothing cute would fit my fat body. She was sad for
me . . . and so was I. A couple of times, she took me to get
my hair cut, colored or highlighted, and then we'd go out for
lunch. For that one day, or at least a few hours, I would feel
better. It wasn't so much the new hair style, but the relief I
found in the food I ate. I felt the most "okay" when I was filling myself up with food. However it was only temporary. My
negative self-talk would start as soon as I finished eating. I'd
repeat things in my head, like "I can't believe you ate all of
that food. You are such a pig. You are going to be fat forever.
No wonder you don't have a boyfriend. How can you even
stand yourself?" The critical self-talk went on endlessly.

Out of desperation and concern, my mom started taking
me to her "healer" friends. She belonged to a metaphysical
study group, "New Agers" back then, that would meet once
a week to learn about different spiritual and metaphysical
teachings. They were a diverse group of people, and each one
had his or her own special gift. They introduced me to many
new subjects, such as astrology, numerology, hypnotherapy,
and crystals. I liked it all so much. I took a couple of classes

and soon realized that I had a real passion for numbers. This is where, twenty-six years ago, my own personal spiritual study truly began.

The group also suggested that I go lie on a bed of crystals at one of the women's houses. I was desperate to feel better, so I agreed to go, even though it felt weird to me. I didn't understand how crystals would help me heal, but then again, what did I know! I lay down on the crystal bed she had created in her living room, and, at first, I did feel some energy, but nothing that made me feel noticeably better. I had already made up my mind that it couldn't work. So, of course, it didn't work. Nothing worked; nothing made me feel any better. I was searching for something outside myself to make me better instead of working through the pain and going within by calling on my Angels. What I thought worked for me was approval, good grades, buying friendships, and a midnight snack.

I continued to earn attention and friendship through material goods. I had everything a sixteen-year-old kid could want, except confidence and self-worth. I would buy my friends gifts, movie tickets, clothes, and dinners. It felt good at times, but I also knew that most of my friends were only friends because I was buying them gifts or paying their way.

On some level, I knew it was my own lack of self-worth that allowed people to take advantage of me. I didn't want to own it nor take responsibility for it, so instead, I blamed the people closest to me: my parents. Even though I had previously had a close relationship with my dad, he teased me daily. He teased me about my weight, the size of my legs, my glasses—you name it, he teased me about it. I blamed him for his controlling behavior, lack of compassion, and negative comments. They all hurt, and he wasn't aware enough to notice. My mom, on the other hand, was very aware. She always knew what I needed, was compassionate and gentle. She was my safe place. She became the referee for my dad and me. However, I blamed her, too, for not being a better example of self-love and for being too nice. If my parents were different, I thought, then maybe I would be different. I found fault in everything outside myself, which was only a projection of what was going on within me. But I did not know how to accept and take responsibility for what was going on inside me. I couldn't even look at it; it was just too much.

I operated from the patterns I had learned as a child and was therefore critical of the people around me and judgmental of myself. Finally, at age nineteen, after manifesting one negative situation after another, I was given the gift of insight through a book called *You Can Heal Your Life*, by Louise Hay. At first I resisted the lessons in the book, but as I continued to dig myself deeper and deeper into a hole of self-pity, I surrendered and began to do the work. By this time, I had manifested a boyfriend who drank often, a child, and was living on welfare and food stamps. The questioning of my self-worth that had begun at age six continued to permeate every aspect of my life.

I began to follow *You Can Heal Your Life* as if it were my Bible. I placed all of my hope in the words of this book. If Louise Hay could begin to love herself, then why not me? I began with saying positive affirmations at least one thousand times a day. I wrote letters, released emotions, visualized a new life, and went back to my passion of learning. I soaked up everything I could get my hands on. Little by little, I noticed that my mood started to improve. I began loving my faults and seeing the world through the eyes of love. The sun seemed a little brighter, the stars a bit shinier, and my heart lighter. I knew I was just beginning, but I was already feeling stronger, kinder, and more loving of myself.

Louise suggested that one of the ways in which you can learn to see the beauty within is to do mirror work. I looked into the mirror each day and connected with my own eyes. As I did this, I repeated positive affirmations, such as "I love and accept myself; I am beauty; I am light; I am divine; I am a loving being capable of receiving love; I am open to receive; I trust my choices"; etc. I said as many positive affirmations as I could think of, and, over time, this exercise softened my heart and allowed me to see the beauty within. (When you have a minute, try this exercise yourself and see how power-ful it is.)

It took me years of intense work to get to a place where I felt my own innate value. Archangel Jophiel was always there to support me, but once again, the lack of self-worth kept me from seeing the beauty. I walked through many pain-ful experiences before I was willing to let go of resistance. But the gift of the energy of Archangel Jophiel is his ability to transform. All through my childhood and early adult life, Archangel Jophiel's energy was present and guiding me in my preferences—preference for the things I did and did not want. And once I was aware of those preferences, I was able to transform my thoughts and beliefs to support them.

VALUE OF THE EXPERIENCE: When you see through eyes of beauty, the things you see are beautiful. When you listen with ears of beauty, the sounds and words you hear are beautiful. When you feel beauty within you, you radiate that beauty all around you. And when you know that you are a beautiful being of love and think thoughts that align with that vibration, you allow others to know the same about themselves.

Archangel Chamuel

Pronounced SHAM-you-el, it means "He who sees or seeks God." Chamuel is the Archangel of unconditional love and adoration.

HELPS WITH: Career, life purpose, finding lost items, building and strengthening relationships, world peace, and seeking soul mates.

COLOR VIBRATION: Pink

GEMSTONES: Rose Quartz, Rhodochrosite, Pink Rhodonite

INVOCATION: I invoke the unconditional love and light of Archangel Chamuel. Please heal any and all emotional wounds or pain that hold me back from truly loving myself as the divine Spirit that I am. Archangel Chamuel, please help me to open my heart to the beauty within me as well as around me. Allow me to see myself through your angelic vibration and feel love as I release any and all resentments, fears, and pain. I ask to experience forgiveness, self-acceptance, and unconditional self-love. Thank you for helping me attract positive, kind, gentle, and nonjudgmental love into myself and my life . . . and so it is!

As I invoke Archangel Chamuel, I imagine a vibrant pink energy surrounding my entire physical being. As I breathe in,

I see that pink energy moving into my heart and filling me with unconditional love and the gentle energy of Archangel Chamuel.

PERSONAL EXPERIENCE: I was first introduced to the energy of Chamuel through a rose quartz stone. I was raised in a metaphysical household in Salt Lake City, Utah, where, at the time, the population was 85 percent Mormon. (It is now 66 percent.) Many of my day-in and day-out struggles centered on being raised in a religiously dominated society that I was not a part of. I found it challenging to grow up in a religious environment that felt so judgmental of others' beliefs and ways of living. Throughout my younger years, I was taught to trust my intuition and let it be my guide, so religion, from very early on, was not for me. I also lacked any kind of challenge in school, because I always felt more aware of what I was being taught than the teachers were. I also struggled with friends—making them and keeping them— and therefore I did not feel like I fit into any part of society. I felt like an outsider, and although I had a few friends, I never felt normal. So my protective walls went up, and I used food as a form of protection and comfort.

My mother, an intuitive herself, could see my day-to-day struggles. She felt my pain and sensed that I needed some help, so she consulted with her metaphysical friends. They had taught my mom about crystals and how different ones can be used for healing. They specifically introduced her to rose quartz and suggested that she buy some for me to carry. Rose quartz is a heart-healing gemstone and is used for treating any issue that needs emotional healing. So my mom asked me to carry this crystal in my pocket at all times.

At the time, I didn't understand how a gemstone was going to make me feel better, but I so desperately wanted to feel better that I did it. I always had one with me and sometimes carried an extra one in my bra.

After a while, I began to notice that if I held the crystal in my hand or rubbed it between my fingers, I felt better. I wanted to share it with my friends, but I knew they would think my entire family and I were weird. But it did bring me peace, and for that I was grateful. As the years progressed and I began to live life, I forgot about some of the tools that had helped me. It was only when self-love and worthiness issues surfaced that I would remember about the rose quartz gemstone. At thirty years old, while enrolled in a program to become a Certified Spiritual Counselor and obtain a Master of Religious Science degree, I experienced an event that changed my awareness of self-love forever.

During one of the classes, I was introduced to a set of tools designed to create, develop, and maintain my relationship with the Angels. I was excited about this, because even though the energy of the angelic realm was familiar to me, working with them was not a part of my daily practice. Throughout my life, and especially in times of trouble, I called upon them but never in a consistent way. So I looked forward to deepening and strengthening my relationship with them.

Over the next several months, my relationship with my Angels evolved and grew. One day in class, I was asked to do an exercise similar to the one I shared with you at the beginning of this book (Developing Your Personal Relationship with Each Archangel in section 2). Just as I suggested earlier that it is helpful to let your intuition guide you in choosing the colors of the week, I let my intuition guide me in choosing an Archangel to work with for a two-week time frame. I was guided to Archangel Chamuel, the angel of unconditional love and adoration. This was the perfect time to work with his energy, since we were heading into the Christmas holiday season. I was excited!

Our specific assignment was to invoke one Archangel and work with his energy. The teacher encouraged us to use a wide variety of techniques, such as carrying the specific stone that is associated with each vibration, wearing the color that the particular Archangel vibrates to, visualizing the Archangel's energy surrounding us, or praying for the Archangel to show us a sign. At the end of each day, we were to journal about our experience. This was a wonderful way to create a personal relationship with each Archangel, as it was based on individual experience rather than another's perception.

I began by asking for guidance and support from Archangel Chamuel. I asked to connect with Chamuel's energy and to learn and feel what unconditional love felt like for myself and then to be able to share that feeling with others. I asked to be an instrument of *love*, to see love, feel love, hear love, and know love in each and every moment. In my meditation, I visualized the color pink flowing through my entire body then extending out to the neighborhood, city, county, state, country, world, and finally the Universe. I visualized this flow every day and wore pink colors and carried a rose quartz stone to intensify Chamuel's energy. I also began affirming that I loved myself, even in moments of doubt. I completely immersed myself in this exercise, and I opened myself up to receive and experience the unconditional love that I had longed for most of my life. I had no idea what any of this would look like or how it would manifest, but I wanted to experience "it" fully.

Within the first few hours of connecting with Archangel Chamuel, I was inspired to be a "Secret Santa," or what I referred to as a "Pixie." A Pixie or Secret Santa is someone who chooses to give a person support anonymously, through gift-giving, money, energy, etc. Once I felt guided to be a Pixie, I asked Spirit whom I was to "pixie," and I very clearly heard the name Kelly, another student in my class—and so began the twelve days of Christmas, Sunny/Pixie style.

Each morning, I woke up and asked Archangel Chamuel to guide me to the perfect gift that would show Kelly love, adoration, and/or joy. I patiently waited for the guidance, since I did not know Kelly very well. I trusted that the Angels would not let me down. Each day became a fun, heart-opening opportunity, not only for me but for my entire family, as well.

The notes I left on Kelly's door each day began, *Dearest Kelly! With loving kindness, From Your PIXIE!* Then each successive day, I added a new line:

> On the 1st day of Christmas my Pixie gave to me,
> Candles to light my way!

> On the 2nd day of Christmas my Pixie gave to me,
> a Cozy Warm Robe, Slippers, and a Cup of Coffee!

> On the 3rd day of Christmas my Pixie gave to me,
> a Bountiful Basket of Bath Goodies!

On the 4th day of Christmas my Pixie gave to me,
Something Soft, Snuggly, and Cozy and Something Shiny!

On the 5th day of Christmas my Pixie gave to me,
Five GOLDEN Books!

On the 6th day of Christmas my Pixie gave to me,
a Basket Full of LOVE and GOODIES!

On the 7th day of Christmas my Pixie gave to me,
a Box of Bedtime Glee!

On the 8th day of Christmas my Pixie gave to me,
Beautiful Roses and a Friendship Ficus Tree!

On the 9th day of Christmas my Pixie gave to me,
Fountains and Fairies for the Gallery!

On the 10th day of Christmas my Pixie gave to me,
Towels, Kerchiefs, and Hankies!

On the 11th day of Christmas my Pixie gave to me,
Nutritional Staples O' Plenty!

On the 12th day of Christmas my Pixie gave to me,
Christmas Decorations and Trees Overflowing!

I spent a lot of time and energy in the vibration of love. There were days when, after I'd dropped off the gift, I felt inspired to go back and leave a little note of encouragement at her doorstep. I was really allowing myself to experience love and be guided by my intuition and the messages from Chamuel. One morning, I woke up and got the hit that Kelly needed a robe and a pair of slippers. So I purchased a pink robe and slippers and left them on the doorstep for her. I wrote a poem about staying warm and cozy and reminded her to love herself unconditionally. A couple days later, I felt guided to purchase a ficus tree and two dozen pink roses. I left these at my favorite spot by the door and wrote another poem about true love and how important it is to have someone in your life who loves you unconditionally.

Each day I looked forward to showing and expressing unconditional love for someone I didn't know very well. I reached out and included others in the fun. A couple of my closest classmates got involved, my husband and kids, and even a yard-maintenance man who was working outside Kelly's house pitched in. It became a game for me. I would drop the various gifts off at random times throughout the day or night and then run and hide so Kelly would not see who her Pixie was.

It was Friday evening when I decided to leave a giant teddy bear for Kelly. A classmate of mine purchased the teddy bear, and she agreed to help deliver the bear that night. The bear was four feet tall, and we felt guided to hang a necklace around the neck. Before the bear was delivered, we both felt guided to leave some money as well, which we did. In addition to the bear, I had wanted to bring a stocking full of dog treats and toys, because I knew Kelly had a dog that she loved dearly. Kelly's dog was like her own child, and I did not want to leave something that important to Kelly out of this experience of unconditional love. However, as we were preparing to deliver her gifts, I got a very strong sense that this was not the right time to leave the dog treats. At first, I thought this feeling was odd because I felt so strongly to give the treats, but I listened to the guidance I was receiving in that moment and did not leave them. I was being given an opportunity to practice listening to my intuitive guidance moment by moment, even though I did not understand why I was feeling that way.

My home, my heart, and my Spirit were filled to the brim with joy as I listened to the guidance of Chamuel. I would ask, and then almost immediately, I would receive an answer. Throughout the two weeks, I made it clear to everyone, including my Angels, that I did not want Kelly to know who her "Pixie" was. I wanted to be anonymous. I also wanted to experience what it felt like to be a physical vessel of unconditional love and to trust the guidance I was receiving from my Angels.

The twelfth day came, and it was Christmas Eve. Our assignment was quickly coming to an end, and I was sad. I wasn't ready for this experience to be over. I enjoyed it so much. Then I was guided to give Kelly one more gift, a Christmas day gift, which made it lucky number thirteen. Around midnight on Christmas Eve, my husband and I drove to Kelly's house and left a porcelain doll on her doorstep. (The doll wore a patchwork-type dress that was torn and tattered, but the message that came with it was special to me. The message conveyed that it didn't matter what the outside looked like, because some of the most precious gifts are found on the inside, hidden behind tears and tatters.) The message and patched dress reminded me of a song, "Coat of Many Colors" by Dolly Parton. If you are not familiar with this song, the lyrics speak about love in the heart and remind us that even though you may not have all the money in the world, you can always have love. So that song ran through my head as I left the doll on the front step. I felt like Santa, my heart full of joy, as I imagined Kelly opening up this last gift on Christmas morning.

As we drove home, it suddenly hit me. The two-week exercise with Archangel Chamuel was over, and I now knew what the energy of absolute unconditional love felt like in my heart, body, mind, and Spirit. I was amazed, blessed, and a little sad for it to be at an end. It was time to get back to "regular" life, so to speak, but I promised myself that I was going to find a way to bring this feeling of love into my regular life!

A few days after Christmas, I received a call from one of my classmates. She was a friend of Kelly's and was aware of what was going on in Kelly's life. She shared with me that on the Friday night that we left the bear, Kelly had tripped and fallen on her dog. The dog was so severely injured that he had to be put down by the vet that evening. Kelly was heartbroken and full of guilt as she left the vet's office. When Kelly returned home, the first thing she saw was the teddy bear on the front doorstep. That night, she cried herself to sleep holding the teddy bear. It helped her feel safe and eased the pain of the loss of her dog, her best friend. The money that we left was exactly the right amount she needed to pay for putting the dog down. But what I never would have suspected, and my classmate shared with me, was that while Kelly was driving home from the vet, she had felt so much guilt and despair that the only way she knew how to feel better was to take her own life. She had planned to kill herself when she got home. *But*, when she came home and saw the bear and the envelope, she was reminded that someone, somewhere in this world *loved* her. She didn't know who or why she was receiving these gifts, all she knew was that someone loved her enough to show up every single day and bring her gifts. Kelly had said that it was this *love* that encouraged her to live through the pain and guilt of the loss of her dog. If there was someone out there who loved her this much, there must be something in her worth loving and maybe, just maybe, she could love herself enough to get through the next horrific days.

There is a quote by Pierre Pradervand that says: "To bless all without distinction is the ultimate form of giving, because those you bless will never know from whence came the sudden ray that burst through the clouds of their skies, and you will rarely be a witness to the sunlight in their lives."

My interpretation of this is that, oftentimes, we do not realize what our blessings can do for someone else. I felt this in my experience with Archangel Chamuel. I was in *love* with life and the energy I was feeling through the blessings I was giving to Kelly. I'd had *no* idea how this experience had affected Kelly's life.

I share this story with you because I want you to remember that Archangel Chamuel is the Angel of unconditional love and that, often, we don't know the power of what we do, the words we speak, or the acts we impart to others.

This experience was one of the most joyous times of my life, and I hadn't known the impact that it was having on Kelly's life. It was fun and loving for me, but it was lifesaving *love* for her. So, if you would like to learn to love yourself and others unconditionally, I encourage you to create a connection with Archangel Chamuel.

VALUE OF THE EXPERIENCE: When you ask the Archangels to allow you to be an instrument of *love*, the *love* is felt, within you as well as all around you. Oftentimes, that *love* will manifest in ways that you may never, ever see or know!

Archangel Gabriel

Pronounced GAY-bree-uhl, it means "God is my strength." Gabriel is the Archangel of communication and is known as the Messenger Angel.

HELPS WITH: Communication in any area, TV and radio work, adoption, child conception and fertility, journalism and writing.

COLOR VIBRATION: White

GEMSTONES: Moonstone, Clear Quartz

INVOCATION: I now invoke the mighty and powerful Archangel Gabriel and his energy of communication and strength. Please bring me insight and awareness so that I may always speak my truth. Remove all doubts and fears, and allow me to express myself in a loving way through body, mind, and Spirit. Please help me to share my words in a way that is gentle, kind, and loving. Please help me to communicate from my heart. Thank you . . . and so it is.

As I invoke Archangel Gabriel's energy, I visualize the white light of Gabriel coming down from the heavens and entering my body through my head. As I sit in this energy, I feel clarity about communication in my throat area, and I say thank you, out loud, to allow that clear communication to move completely through me.

PERSONAL EXPERIENCE: About fifteen years ago, I learned about Archangel Gabriel, the Angel of communication and the one to call on for support and guidance when you need to be clearly understood. He is also the Angel of conception, fertility, and adoption. Archangel Gabriel's energy was most prevalent in my life when I was struggling to have my second child. It is the energy of Archangel Gabriel that I believe supported my dream to be a mother again after suffering three miscarriages.

In the fall of 1993, I discovered I was pregnant a month before my fiancé, Brett, and I were to be married. I was surprised, to say the least. We wanted to have a child together—it would be my second—but hadn't planned on it happening quite so soon. My immediate emotion was fear. I was afraid of losing my life during childbirth as I had almost done with my first son Crew. I immediately went to the doctor, and he administered all kinds of medical tests. At eight weeks pregnant, my body was already starting to show signs of toxemia which would likely turn into pre-eclampsia, and I was advised to have a medical termination. Even though I wanted another child, my fiancé and I weren't willing to risk my life, so two weeks before my wedding, they performed a medical termination, and I lost my baby.

Eighteen months later, after much thought and contemplation about the risks, we purposely tried to have a baby. We were immediately successful, and this time I decided to see a new doctor who specialized in high-risk pregnancies. I was monitored very closely, and my body seemed to be responding well at six and eight weeks. I was excited. I could finally start buying baby clothes, and I was enjoying every moment of it. At twelve weeks, we got to listen to the heartbeat. It sounded strong and healthy. I was relieved and happy to be past the scary part. However, my doctor was cautious and had me come in every two weeks for a follow-up. At fourteen weeks, I felt as though something was off. I couldn't explain it, but something wasn't right. I asked the doctor to do an ultrasound. At that time, they did not typically do an ultrasound that early, but, given my history, my doctor agreed. I immediately went in for the test. Ultrasounds were not new to me, as I'd had more than twenty of them with my first son. I was devastated to see that there was no heartbeat. Sometime between twelve and fourteen weeks, my child had died. Why me? Why now? What did I do to deserve this?

My doctor advised me that I would miscarry naturally within a week or so. I was having so many emotions surrounding that thought. How do I just wait for my dead baby to come out? I couldn't do it. I called the doctor a couple days later and we agreed to do a D&C (dilation and curettage) to remove the baby. So at fifteen weeks, I went in for surgery. During the procedure, there were some problems, and I had considerable bleeding. Over the next three months, they had to do five more D&Cs just to get the bleeding to permanently stop. It was hell. I was mad at the world, God, the Universe . . . you name it. When I didn't want a baby at age eighteen, I was able to carry one to term and birthed my first son Crew. Now I was in a loving, healthy relationship with my husband, yet I just suffered my second loss. *Why?*

The doctor suggested fertility testing to see if there was a problem with my husband or me. We gave blood, had more tests done, and did a sperm count; everything looked just fine.

It must be me. I knew it had to be me. I was completely overwhelmed. This was my punishment for not being the mom that I "should" have been to my son Crew. I was at a loss as to how to cope with my feelings; so, instead, I went back on birth-control pills and threw myself into everyday life.

My focus became being the best housekeeper, wife, and mother I could. I tried to convince myself that having one son would make me happy, but those words never felt right. I knew somewhere deep in my soul that there was one more baby I was meant to have, I just didn't believe it would happen. I would pray that the pain and sadness would go away, but I never thought to ask Gabriel to help me. I never even asked Raphael to help heal the emotions and physical issues that were causing me to struggle with maintaining a pregnancy. I think I wanted it soooooo badly that I forgot to use my tools, and, once again, the issue of worthiness reared its ugly head. I realized that I didn't feel as if I deserved the help.

So I disregarded my soul yearning and focused on taking care of my son Crew and my husband Brett. My son was a challenge, so it was a *big* job. I did this for another year and a half, and one day, I just simply changed my mind. I decided to try to get pregnant one more time and went off birth control. It worked! Within the first month I was pregnant.

Again, I was nervous throughout the pregnancy. I was very afraid that I would lose another baby. I had already lost two. Was I strong enough to make it through another loss? I called my doctor if I felt even a little bit "off." She was very supportive and seemed to understand my fears. I went in for an office visit every two weeks, and each time she assured me the heartbeat was strong. This one looked like a keeper. I wanted to believe her, but again, my intuition told me differently.

At twelve weeks I felt cramping while walking Crew to school. When I got home, I noticed I was bleeding. I panicked and called the doctor. She told me to lie down and relax and that it was probably just a little spotting. However, that feeling, that knowing, moved through me as I lay on the couch, telling the doctor that I was going to lose this one, too. I went into the office that afternoon, and she confirmed what I already knew. My baby had died, I was miscarrying again.

This time, I had a different reaction. I was still sad, but I knew that this baby was not meant to be with me. Something had shifted within me. I realized, for the first time, that I hadn't felt as if I *deserved* to have another baby. This was an "aha!" moment for me. I had been in so much fear throughout all of the pregnancies, no wonder I couldn't carry the babies to term. This pregnancy and the brief time that this baby was with me was a gift. I was reminded to see myself as a full-term pregnant woman. Although I was sad at the loss of another child, this time I felt very clear on the subject of babies. I knew that if I was going to have one, then I needed to change my thoughts and my emotions. I needed to let go of the fear that was ruling my every thought. I needed to release the self-judgment and the criticism, and I needed to love myself in the same way that any mother who was bringing a new baby into this world would.

I asked for help. I asked the Angels to surround me, guide me, and support me. I asked them to help me to heal, to love myself again, and to help me bring back the love that I knew was within me but had not been honoring. I didn't specifically ask Gabriel for his help at this time, but I did ask the Angels to help release any patterns that were holding me back from experiencing the joy of motherhood, on all levels, and having a healthy pregnancy.

Two months later I was pregnant again. I knew this one was going to stick. I just *knew* it.

I was ready! I released, asked for help, and had my Angels, guides, and spiritual team supporting me. I knew "we" were going to be okay. However, eight weeks into the pregnancy, I started bleeding. I was hysterical. How could I have been wrong again? I started second-guessing my intuition. But, as I drove to the doctor's office, a gentle voice from within reminded me to be calm, that it was all right, we were going to be okay. Once I arrived at the office, I requested that the doctor see if there was a heartbeat. She assured me it was strong. I felt a little relief. We agreed to try a few new therapies and make some dietary changes.

I began a new type of progesterone therapy, and she told me to begin eating meat, which was very difficult for me as I had been a vegetarian for more than six years. She felt that I needed the additional protein and iron found in red meats. She also suggested that I go on bed rest for a few weeks. She then sent me home to relax and visualize my healthy baby. I complied with all of the suggestions, and, after that initial scare, I sailed through the rest of my pregnancy.

It was a beautiful, amazing, wonderful experience—I was so excited! I had a healthy pregnancy and had gained fifty pounds by my eighth month, which was a great sign. I was feeling amazing and was looking forward to a traditional natural birth. We had a birth plan in place, had taken all of the classes, and were ready to create a different birth experience from the one I'd had with my first son. This time, I would be the creator of my experience.

All during this time, I continued to connect and communicate with my Angels and guides daily. By specifically asking for help with my pregnancy, I believe that Archangel Gabriel became my guardian. The next experience is evidence of that!

August 25, 1997, is a date I will never forget. It was three weeks before my son was due, and that morning I had woken up with an absolute knowing that something was wrong. Looking back, I believe that Archangel Gabriel was communicating with me through my thoughts. I called the doctor in a panic and tried to convince her that I knew something was wrong. I begged her to let me come in and see her. She said she had just seen me the week before and that everything was fine. She also told me that she was getting ready to leave on her honeymoon for two weeks. I wouldn't take no for an answer. I insisted that something was wrong and that I had the same feeling that I'd had with all the other lost pregnancies. I told her that I wanted to schedule a C-section before she went out of town. This took her by surprise, as I had been very insistent on having a VBAC (vaginal birth after Caesarean). She told me it was too early to do that, and I needed to wait at least one week. She would contact me when she got back from her honeymoon, and we would go from there. As I hung up the phone, I was shaking. I was so scared I didn't know what to do. I lay on the couch and cried and cried.

About half an hour later, the phone rang, and it was the doctor. She said, "Sunny, there is something about your mother's intuition that I have to believe, so I will do the C-section on the twenty-seventh or twenty-eighth; which day do you want?" I was so happy, and a sense of peace fell over me. I sat for a moment and asked Spirit which day was best. The twenty-seventh would be the perfect day to give birth to my son—Mother Teresa's true birthday.

On August 27, 1997, my second son, Arizona Blue Johnston, was delivered by Caesarean section at 1:47 p.m. The umbilical cord was wrapped twice around his neck, and he was completely blue and lifeless. The nurses and doctors rushed to get oxygen flowing into his body, and within two minutes, bit by bit, his tiny little blue body started turning pink. His color changed from the top of his head to the bottom of his feet. It was as if Spirit were blowing life into him, and it was amazing to watch. It was a miracle! He was alive!

He was alive and breathing because Archangel Gabriel had communicated clearly to me, and I had listened. I will forever be grateful to the amazing energy of this Archangel and the power all the Angels have to help us see and hear clearly.

VALUE OF THE EXPERIENCE: When you ask for help, remember to listen—in all ways. Listen to the subtle messages as well as the strong messages. When listened to and acted upon, these messages can literally save a life!

Archangel Raphael

Pronounced RAH-fee-uhl, it means "God heals" or "God has healed." Raphael is the Archangel of healing. Raphael heals physical bodies as well as mental, emotional, and spiritual bodies.

HELPS WITH: Eliminating or reducing addictions and cravings, healing on all levels, guidance and support for healers, physical and spiritual eyesight, clairvoyance, and finding lost pets.

COLOR VIBRATION: Green

GEMSTONES: Jade, Aventurine

INVOCATION: I ask Archangel Raphael to surround me in his healing vibration of emerald-green light. I am in need of healing at this time, and I ask that you infuse me with your healing energy. Please surround me and fill me with health, well-being, and wholeness. Help me to heal any wounds—physical, mental, emotional, or spiritual—from the past or present. Heal and restore every aspect of my being for the highest good of all . . . and so it is!

As I invoke Archangel Raphael's energy, I see the emerald-green energy completely surrounding my body. I feel this energy moving within me, and I affirm that I am healthy and whole and that well-being is my divine birthright.

PERSONAL EXPERIENCE: The loving healing energy of Archangel Raphael saved my life. Yes, I said, saved my life. Raphael stood beside me as my most challenging physical healing occurred twenty-one years ago. This physical healing began with my pregnancy at the age of eighteen.

I had not planned to have a baby, not ever. Thoughts of an abortion crossed my mind, and I was even encouraged to have one, but when faced with the decision, I could not do it. At some deep level, I knew I was meant to have the baby, even though on the surface, I felt it was not right.

So, at age eighteen, I found myself pregnant and in a relationship with someone who drank daily, and, as you might expect, this posed many challenges. The energy that was present in our relationship was also fueled by lack: lack of money, lack of self-esteem, and lack of self-worth. This kind of energy is very heavy, and because I was not protecting my own energy, I suffered. On an energetic level, I was getting weaker and weaker, and the heaviness began to take a toll on me physically, mentally, and emotionally.

During the fourth month of my pregnancy, I developed severe toxemia, which eventually led to eclampsia: pregnancy-induced high blood pressure. The doctors prescribed strong medication for the high blood pressure and recommended complete bed rest for the remainder of my pregnancy. And when I say complete bed rest, I *mean* complete bed rest. The only time I could get out of bed was to use the restroom or to go to my doctor's appointments, which were every other day. My child and I were at severe risk for seizures and liver and kidney damage, and the doctors felt bed rest would help minimize those complications. Bed rest did not sit very well with me; I am an Aries and like to go, go, go. However, something inside me knew. I could hear this whisper of a voice within me, offering to help, but I refused to allow it.

I didn't believe I deserved help. I'd made a big mistake, and this was my punishment. All my critical thinking could say was, "Sunny, you have been a very bad girl, and because of it, you now have six months to lie in this bed and think about it. You have all morning, afternoon, and evening to think about what you might have done differently."

I felt guilty, ashamed, embarrassed, humiliated, stupid, and many other negative vibrations. It was these feelings that created the toxicity in my mind that eventually manifested in my body. Today, I am very aware of how my thoughts create, but back then, all I could recognize was that I felt scared.

For the next six months, these toxic feelings continued. I alternated between feelings of depression, rage, frustration, and boredom. I cried during the times in which I had the courage to acknowledge my situation. Thoughts of "How did I end up here?" and "Why me?" frequently attacked my mind. My thoughts were just as toxic as my body, and I continued to exist in this environment for an additional two weeks past my due date. Finally, the doctors induced labor and during my twenty-sixth hour of labor, I had a mild stroke. Time was of the essence, so the doctors performed an emergency C-section; several minutes later, my son was born. I was not able to see him take his first breath since I was unconscious, but the minute I awoke, I felt pure joy as the nurse placed this beautiful baby boy in my arms. We had both made it through the hard part—at least that is what I thought.

Three days after my son's birth, I developed a low-grade fever. I was feeling out of sorts and not recovering the way I should. Within hours, the low-grade fever turned into a high-grade fever of 106. I broke out in hives all over my upper body, and the doctors discovered that I was oozing pus from my incision. They were uncertain of the source of the infection, so they decided to go back in surgically to see if a sponge or instrument had been left inside; however, they found nothing. They had no explanation for the infection that ran rampant in my body. I was in severe physical pain, as well as emotional pain. I had seen my son for only a brief amount of time, and he was now at home and being cared for by my parents. I could not see him again because the doctors feared that I was contagious. I felt very alone . . . yet I still did not listen to that whisper of a voice within. I knew I could ask my Angels for help and healing, and, because of past experiences, I did believe they could help me. But I did not feel deserving, and that lack of worthiness kept me from asking. So I continued on in pain and in resistance of the spiritual guidance that was inside me.

Much of the time that I was in the hospital, I was detached from my physical body. It was such a painful place to be, the only way I found relief was to check out. I remember floating above my body and watching the nurses scrub the infection that had taken over my lower torso and upper thighs. Not many friends or family came to visit. I was very lonely and afraid, and I didn't want to die. How could I get through this all by myself?

The doctors continued to search for answers to the mysterious infection. They pumped me full of double and triple doses of antibiotics and performed an additional surgery to see if the source could be viewed from inside. Nothing! The 106-degree fever persisted, and I was getting weaker and weaker. The doctors finally admitted that they could do nothing to help me and asked me to sign away the rights to my son. They did not know how much longer I would live. Upon hearing those words, I felt stunned and shocked. My mind began racing. All I did was have a baby. I was young and healthy, and *all I did was have a baby*. How could my life be ending? I couldn't believe it. I refused to believe it. *Now* it was time, and I began to ask for help as I turned to that whisper of a voice within. On the eve of Mother's Day, I heard that voice within say, "I am Archangel Raphael, and I want you to call everyone you know and ask them to pray for you. Ask them to pray in whatever form of religion or belief system they have." So, I called everyone I knew and asked them to pray for me. I had decided that I wanted to live, and I wanted to see my child again. I spent many hours on the telephone, asking and trusting that each person I talked with would be there for me, supporting and holding the vision of wholeness. Twelve hours later (and three hundred-plus dollars in long-distance phone charges) my fever broke, and for the first time in two and a half weeks, I had hope.

It was a miracle. The doctors could not explain the hows and the whys, but I knew. I knew it was the support and prayers of my friends and my family, but most importantly, that voice within, Archangel Raphael. For when I asked, invoked, and allowed the healing energy of Raphael, healing took place. I was open and receptive, and that is what saved my life. That evening I had made a deal with the Universe. I promised to be open and willing if I could just see a sign that I would be okay, that I would really make it through it all. It was the next morning that my fever broke. That was the only sign I needed.

Against doctors' orders—on the day after Mother's Day—I checked myself out of the hospital. I had found another way to heal, and I began trusting in the healing powers of Archangel Raphael. I was a medical miracle, and I continued to work with Archangel Raphael's energy from that day forward. It took me several months to regain my strength and complete health and wholeness. Each day, I visualized an emerald-green energy around me and within me. I continued to ask Archangel Raphael for healing on an emotional and physical level. I asked for healing around the core issue of this illness. Archangel Raphael helped me to see that I had manifested this illness because I was judgmental of myself. I felt unworthy of the unconditional love and acceptance that I needed to feel from within. The only one who can love me as Spirit loves me, is me. And with that knowledge, I began to heal from the inside out. I continued to listen to that whisper and to this day, I am amazed at what messages lie within.

This experience taught me how incredibly powerful Archangel Raphael's healing energy is. Since that time, Raphael has been by my side and continues to support my students and me. Together we are teaching *those who are open* how to find the healing power within and how to work with the powerful energy of Archangel Raphael.

VALUE OF THE EXPERIENCE: When you invoke Archangel Raphael's healing energy and ask for healing with an open heart and mind, you'll receive it. When you allow the healing by opening your heart, you are healed!

Archangel Uriel

Pronounced YOO-ree-uhl, it means "God is Light" or "God's Light." Uriel is the Archangel that illuminates situations, gives prophetic information, and offers transmutation.

HELPS WITH: Insight, clarity, peace, vision, problem solving, writing, new ideas, study, and tests.

COLOR VIBRATION: Ruby Red

GEMSTONES: Amber, Ruby

INVOCATION: I invoke the wise and peaceful energy of Archangel Uriel to completely surround my physical and energetic body. Please help soothe all conflict in my life and replace it with peace, clarity, and insight. I ask you to help me release any mental or emotional patterns that keep me stuck in my fears. I ask that you fill me with the knowingness of who I really am. Please help me to trust my experiences, so I may see the greater vision, understand the value of each, and grow in a way that serves all. I am blessed to be on this journey of life, and I thank you, Uriel, for your continued guidance, wisdom, and vision . . . and so it is!

As I invoke Archangel Uriel's energy of wisdom, I imagine or visualize myself completely enveloped in the color red. I take a deep breath in and see, hear, feel, and know that Archangel Uriel is guiding me throughout my physical journey.

PERSONAL EXPERIENCE: I was unfamiliar with Archangel Uriel's energy, even though I had read about him when I was a teenager. I had not had my own experience with him in a way that I could consciously remember, but looking back now, I realize that many of my thoughts, ideas, and inspirations were being guided by the wise energy of Archangel Uriel.

When you invoke Archangel Uriel's energy or vibration, remember that his energy helps transmute things to a higher form. An example of transmutation would be shifting a negative experience into a positive experience. You may have had a situation in your life that seemed very difficult, and you were unsure of how it was going to turn out, but in the process, you learned about trust. So this became a positive experience. Archangel Uriel will also help us transmute lower vibrational energies into higher, enlightened spiritual understanding, turn disappointments into victories, and find blessings in adversity.

Archangel Uriel is often referred to as the Angel of illumination. He helps us see the bigger picture and often guides us with prophetic information. Being able to see the bigger picture, while in the midst of a difficult situation, can help you make decisions that are for the highest good for all involved. This was the case for me when Crew's paternal grandmother had a stroke.

The day started like many others, but several miraculous events occurred, and they all began with a phone call from Crew's birth father, John. I hadn't talked to him for a couple of years, so I was surprised when he called. He told me that his mom had had a stroke, and they were going to take her off life support. She had very little brainstem activity, was in a coma, and the doctors thought she would transition immediately after the life support was disconnected. I began feeding my youngest son, Arizona, his breakfast, and my heart sank as I listened to John talk. Delores, my former mother-in-law, and I had definitely had our ups and downs. John and I had lived in a shack adjacent to her garage when I was pregnant with Crew, and there were many times when we irritated each other.

She always wanted what little money we had for electricity and the phone bill. I was so angry with her that, at times, I blamed her for her son's incompetence. But after I moved away, Delores and I became quite close. We talked on the phone every couple of weeks, and I would share with her how Crew was doing. She loved Crew and me very much, and we loved her, too.

She was a different kind of lady. She spoke with a gruff tone, complained about everything, and smoked at least two packs of cigarettes a day. When I first met her, she was taken aback by me. She was a little jealous of me, since I was dating her youngest child. Although he was nineteen, she wasn't quite ready to let go of the attention he always had for his mom. Years later, we laughed about this, but in the beginning, they were obstacles.

Delores was a hard worker. She raised six kids basically on her own. She struggled financially and emotionally, but she was one strong woman. She had amazing inner strength. She loved her animals and her plants. I would always find her outside watering her plants. Her common saying was that they were bone dry—this still makes me smile—bone dry. I always felt she received the unconditional love she was always looking for from Mother Earth and her animals. I believe she knew that on some level as well.

She lived a difficult life. She channeled all of her hurts and pain into poetry; she was as gifted a poet as they come. She was strong and tough on the outside, but I remember seeing her in the wee dark hours of the morning, drinking her coffee and smoking her cigarettes while writing. She would write poem after poem until it grew light outside. Oftentimes the words spoke of sunrises and the beauty of Mother Earth. She expressed her own emotions and feelings through words and nature.

As the years went by, Delores and I developed an even stronger relationship. She talked to me about her life and her struggles to keep her kids fed. She had to be tough to live through raising six children and having an alcoholic husband. He had left many years earlier, when her kids were still young, which left her with quite a bit of resentment. I remember her telling me the story of when he'd come home drunk one night and was angry about something. She took the three youngest kids, went into the desert, and slept under some sagebrush, hoping he wouldn't find her. This was just one of many stories that left her and her children haunted with pain. This pain was often expressed through addictions, and many of her children would struggle with their own addiction issues.

I remember that shortly before Delores left this physical world, she shared with me intimate details about her life, her frustrations with herself as a mother and with her children. She wished she could have done some things differently. I tried to reassure her that we do the best we can with what we know and what we have to work with. She would usually just respond with a sigh. That was the Delores I knew and loved.

After John called, I was very upset. My heart was broken. I wanted to be there to tell her goodbye, but there was no time. The doctors thought she would pass immediately after they unplugged the machine. As I sat on the floor crying, I felt a sense of sadness yet hopefulness. I couldn't explain it. I tried to finish feeding Arizona, but I couldn't focus. I turned on the TV for him, *Blue's Clues,* and went in my room to meditate and pray. As I sat in my chair, I kept asking to know if Delores had passed. Because of our strong bond, I thought I would be able to feel her Spirit leave this earthly plane. I really had no basis for that, because I'd never been with anyone who passed, but that is how I felt.

An hour later, I still had not heard from John, so I tried to call him. I couldn't reach anyone. At first, I was angry because I thought she had died and no one had called me. Then I was angry because I didn't feel anything when she passed away. If the doctors had said she would pass immediately, I must have not been tuned in if I couldn't feel her leave.

In the midst of trying to sort this out, another sense came over me. Aha. I knew it. She was waiting for me! At first it didn't make any sense. That thought went against everything John had told me, but I just kept hearing inside my head: "She is waiting for me."

I finally reached someone at one of her sons' houses and asked if she had passed yet. He said no, she hadn't. I was confused. Why was no one answering at the care center then? He told me that everyone had left. "What do you mean everyone left? Are you kidding me? She is still alive, and there is no one there to be with her? Why?? Why is no one there with her?" I was in shock! The response shocked me even more. "She is already gone to us. It is just too hard to watch her go, so we came back to the house." I was stunned and angry, yet not surprised. I knew that her children had a fear of death, and I knew it was their way of dealing with the situation; but I was also devastated and upset that she was alone.

I hung up the phone and sat quietly for a minute. I knew

I needed to do something, but I was not sure what to do. It was a six-hour drive, and the doctors had said that she could go any minute. I knew I'd never make it to California in time to be with her; so I let the questions go, I got out of my head and into my heart, and I stayed very still and quiet.

It was then that Archangel Uriel first appeared to me, because the answer was so clear, "Yes, go, Sunny. You will make it; she is waiting for you; you will make it."

I questioned the guidance for a brief moment, as that is my nature, but I knew it was the right thing to do. I couldn't get in touch with my husband, and I knew that time was running out. I called my mom and asked her to come and watch my children. My mom lived two hours away, so it would take her a while to get to my house. I didn't have that kind of time, so I asked my "new" neighbor if she would keep my twenty-month-old child and pick up my other son from school. I asked her if she'd be willing to watch them until my mom got there or my husband got home from work. And then I asked her if she'd tell my husband that I was on a plane to California, and I'd call him tonight to explain everything! I am sure she thought I was crazy. Now, this was a big step for me, because I had never left my children with anyone but family; so to ask a neighbor, actually a complete stranger, was quite unlike me. However, Spirit told me that it would be okay.

I changed my clothes and got on a plane to California. While in flight, I sat next to a man who could tell I was distraught. I shared with him why I was going to California, and I think he asked me questions to keep me distracted from the worry that I might not make it in time. He was an

Angel in disguise. I landed and immediately rented a car. I still had a nearly two-hour drive with no traffic. During the drive, I kept praying that she would wait for me. My Angels kept reminding me, over and over again, that Spirit wouldn't have had me go through all of this and not have her there waiting for me when I got there. I knew there was divine guidance directing my every move; however, every once in a while, my ego would step in for a little visit and I'd freak out. So to calm myself, I turned on the radio; the song "Angel," by Sarah McLachlan, was playing. This made me cry. I felt as if it were validation that she would wait for me. A few minutes later, I changed the channel, and the same song came on again. I was amazed. Okay, I thought. I get the message.

I knew Archangel Uriel was helping me see the bigger picture. He was guiding me to her, and I would be there at the right time. Throughout the long drive, I changed the radio channel six more times and heard that song on every channel. I was in awe of the power of the Universe as I realized that it was I who was in the arms of the Angels, and they were guiding me to Delores.

Finally, I arrived. As I pulled into the parking lot, I took a deep breath, said a prayer to my guides and Angels, and went in. I had never been around someone who was in a coma or about to die. I was worried that I might feel scared, but I wasn't. I felt calmer than I thought I would. A sense of peace filled my body as I walked into the room and saw Delores lying in the bed. I was relieved to see her there, thankful that I had made it, and grateful that she was not going to die alone. The first thing I noticed was that she looked like she was sleeping. She didn't seem to be in any pain. I walked right up to her bed and told her I was there to be with her while she made her transition. I thanked her for waiting for me. I sat on the bed on her left side and just stopped and looked at her. After a few minutes, I left the room because my heart was full of emotion. I questioned myself about being there. My mind told me that I didn't know what to do in this situation and that it was going to be scary, but my heart told me to stay.

I called the house where her children were staying to let them know that I was there. I said I had come to be with her while she passed. They told me I could come over to the house if I wanted to and get something to eat. I declined and told them I planned to stay until she passed away. I felt grief-stricken and outraged that not one of them was with Delores. I went back into her room and sat with her. My mind wondered about the pain she might be in, knowing that none of her children were here.

Suddenly I felt the presence of someone behind me. I turned around and saw John standing in the hallway, crying. I got up and hugged him for at least five minutes. In that embrace, I felt all of the sadness, hurt, and frustration that he was going through.

We continued to hold each other in silence. It was an interesting moment for me. The anger and frustration that I felt toward Delores's family members dissolved, and all that remained was compassion. I understood how difficult this was for him, and I felt the fear of death that had taken him over. We walked down the hallway for a bit and did not say a word. As we neared the exit door, I told him I would call when she had gone. We embraced one last time, and he thanked me.

I went back in her room and spent the next seventeen hours with her. The doctors had said that she would be gone in a matter of minutes, but she was still here. She had waited for me. I felt honored and responsible. I felt so many emotions, including absolute love.

I climbed into her hospital bed and lay down next to her. I put Chapstick on her dry lips. I talked with her and actually felt her talking back to me. I hugged her and held her hand. I told her how much I loved her, how sorry I was that I had moved and taken her grandson Crew away from her. I shared with her how hard I had tried to be a good mom and how hard it had been to leave her son to make a better life. I shared everything and held nothing back. There were long periods of silence in which I just listened to her breathe. The nurse said that her breathing would change and it did—it would be heavy, then light. She would rattle off and on, and then it would be easier again. I finally fell asleep beside her. It was such an incredibly peaceful time.

I woke up an hour later, and a series of events began that told me Delores was preparing to leave. The television came on, and it startled me. I knew from all my metaphysical studies that when Spirit people enter a room, electrical systems sometimes get whacky. I watched her breathing, but nothing happened. So, I turned the television off; about ten minutes later, it came back on. I turned it off again. I began to talk to Delores and tell her that it was okay for her to go. She could leave anytime, and I was staying with her until she did. So, each time the television came on, I thought it was a sign that she was ready to pass. This continued four or five times. Finally, I called the nurse and asked if someone could come and check out the TV. Maybe it wasn't spiritual electricity, maybe it was just simply malfunctioning.

They sent in a repairman, and he checked out everything and said it was fine. But to be sure it didn't happen again, he unplugged the power cable from the wall. He assured me that would take care of it. Well twenty minutes later, it happened again. I called the repairman back in, and we both watched in amazement as the television came on. How could it be? I decided this was a serious sign, and the time that Delores would pass was getting closer. At the same time, I felt the energy in the room change. I thought that her Spirit family members were coming and gathering around her. I couldn't see them, but I was getting chills and feeling the energy move around me.

It was about eight in the morning. I got up and got ready quickly, as I knew she was about to leave, and I didn't want to miss anything. Delores's breathing became slower and slower. The death rattle they had talked about had finally begun after seventeen hours. All of a sudden, I felt scared. I knew I needed to release the fear and trust my Spirit, but I wasn't sure how. I felt out of control because I didn't know what exactly was going to happen. I asked the nurse; she said that Delores's heart would stop, and there would be no more noise. I held Delores's hand and waited.

I asked the Angels to surround us both. I asked for the strength to help me through this next step in our journey. I prayed for her freedom from a physical body that had served her so well. As I continued my prayers, I had my last conversation with Delores. I heard her voice very clearly say, "Sunny, put my eyebrows on. Don't you let me leave here without my eyebrows on." I thought I was going crazy. I didn't know how to put eyebrows on, and in my mind, I said back to Delores, "I don't even have an eyebrow pencil. I can't do it." She responded, "Yes, you can. Don't let me leave without my eyebrows." I giggled a bit. She was in the midst of her transition and was concerned about her brows. I thought to myself, Spirit does have a sense of humor!

As I stayed in this moment, her breathing got louder and slower. I asked the nurse to stay in there with me for an added comfort. I sat back down next to Delores's bed and held her hands in mine. I closed my eyes, and I put my head down by her heart. A few moments later, I felt this powerful, enormous energy rush through my arms at the same time I felt Delores release her physical body. A white-colored energy moved through my hands to the bottom of my feet, then to the top of my head and out my crown.

It is hard to describe this, but the energy felt like a wave moving through me. My entire body started shaking for several minutes and then as quick as it came, it was gone—and so was Delores. Her Spirit left as quickly as the energy that had come in through my hands and left through my crown. I couldn't move. I was present to what had just happened and was in awe. I knew at that moment that something incredible had happened to me that day, but I didn't realize how life changing it would be.

The days following Delores's death were transformational for me. I felt like I *must* get on with my journey. That it was time. I felt like I was being guided from above as well as from within. I know that Archangel Uriel had supported me through the entire forty-eight hours. I believe that Delores is now one of my Spirit Guides, and she has guided me, step by step, to the life that I now live. She "forced" me to face my fears, own my gifts, and speak my truth, and I will be forever grateful to her for giving me such an incredible gift.

VALUE OF THE EXPERIENCE: There is a greater purpose in the midst of chaos, heartache, life changes, and even death. Seeing, feeling, and knowing the greater purpose brings a sense of peace as you walk through the journey of life. Illumination is yours, if you will release the fear.

Archangel Zadkiel

Pronounced ZAHD-key-el, it means "Righteousness of God." Zadkiel is the Archangel of forgiveness, mercy, and benevolence.

HELPS WITH: Forgiveness of self and others, emotional healing, compassion, freedom, finding lost objects, and memory.

COLOR VIBRATION: Violet

GEMSTONE: Amethyst

INVOCATION: I invoke the energy of Archangel Zadkiel. I ask you to surround me in your light of forgiveness and mercy. Please help me to soften my heart so that I may forgive myself and help support me in releasing my pain, bitterness, and negativity. Help me remove any and all obstacles that stand in the way of my connection to the deeper love I know I have within me . . . and so it is!

As I invoke Archangel Zadkiel, I visualize a violet flame just above my head. I imagine this flame absorbing all of the negative thoughts, feelings, and emotions that hold me back from forgiving myself and others. I allow all of the lower vibrational energies to be absorbed by Zadkiel's loving violet energy.

PERSONAL EXPERIENCE: For many years I searched, looking for answers, support, healing, and guidance. My life became a search-and-rescue mission of sorts, but I never found any answers in the places I was looking. I traveled the state of Arizona for information on ADHD, OCD, ODD, autism, and bipolar tendencies, so I could help Crew, who had been diagnosed at the age of seven with them all. I visited doctors, psychologists, healers, chiropractors, past-life regressionists, psychics, naturopaths, hypnotherapists, and energy healers. I tried conventional medicine, holistic therapies, biofeedback, rebirthing, cranio-sacral therapy, massage, nutrition, allergy testing, and even went as far as signing up my son for a trial study at Phoenix Children's Hospital. I was looking for the answer, the magic pill, the miraculous tool that would help him; instead, I finally realized that the answer for his wellness was inside me.

Let me take you back to the beginning, the very beginning of my pregnancy with Crew. I was quite mature for an eighteen-year-old girl. I'd been living with my boyfriend for six months, had been out of school since the age of fifteen, and had been working since age nine. I'd lived a lot of life and had many experiences, but I was *not* ready for a baby. I never, ever planned to have children, so finding myself pregnant at age eighteen was quite a shock. I was full of anger, frustration, sadness, and fear, and my thoughts ran rampant. "Why me? Why was I the one to get caught? What were people going to think of me? Would my boyfriend be able to handle it?" And my deepest fear was what my parents were going to say.

I hid the confirmed pregnancy test in the car. All I wanted was for it to go away. When I showed the test to my best and only friend in California, she reiterated all the questions that had been running through my own mind. It was overwhelming, and I just sat on the trunk of my car and cried. My boyfriend finally came home from work, and I broke the news to him. His first suggestion was to have an abortion. I agreed. There was no way I could have a baby.

A couple of days later, I made an appointment at a local pregnancy counseling center to confirm I was pregnant. I'd convinced myself the night before that the testing kit I'd used was flawed and that a professional medical test would give me the answer I wanted to hear. The staff was kind and courteous and eager to assist me, and I felt supported for the first time since I'd found out. The test results came back, and I was indeed eight weeks pregnant. Fear and panic set in, and I started to talk with the staff about an abortion. They did not seem to be as receptive to my decision as I had hoped. In that moment, as I looked closer at the decor and posters, I realized that I was sitting in a Christian Counseling Center. I was told to watch a little video, and I did. As I watched, I saw pictures of the embryo at all different stages of development. Guilt started to settle in; by the end of the film, I *knew* I was going to have this baby. I couldn't live with the guilt and shame of an abortion, so I chose to have a child.

I became very aware of all facets of my life once I'd made the decision to have this child. I stopped partying with my boyfriend. I realized I was in a situation that was unhealthy for me and my unborn baby. I was very fearful, and I spent most of my days crying about my situation or fighting with my boyfriend. He spent his days leisurely, working once in a while when he felt like it, while I worked a full-time job and paid all of the bills. Then he would stay out all night long, play with his band, spend all of my money, get drunk, and then come home. This was not an environment that I wanted to see my child come into; however, I was trapped in my own emotions.

These emotions were often unexpressed, and my energy became toxic; so toxic, in fact, that four months into my pregnancy, I developed toxemia and pre-eclampsia. This toxic energy was affecting not only me, but my unborn child as well. My baby was growing and developing inside me in the midst of toxic energy, negative emotions, and now physical illness. And while he was growing inside me, I was loving myself less and less and becoming more and more depressed.

Over the next five months, I gave up control of my life. I moved back in with my parents because I needed to be taken care of, and, thank God, my mom was a great caretaker. If not for her, I likely would not have made it. I was on complete bed rest due to the pre-eclampsia and taking medications to maintain my blood pressure; I needed to be monitored daily. I had difficulty lying on my left side day in and day out, but was told that if I did not, then possibly neither of us would survive.

The day finally came, and I was having my baby. I was very anxious. I went to the hospital and they induced labor. During rounds of intense contractions, my blood pressure soared, and I began to have a stroke. One of the last things I can remember was all the monitors going off—the baby and I were in serious trouble. A nurse injected medication into my IV to try to stop the stroke as they rushed my bed down the hallway. I could hear them saying, as I drifted in and out of consciousness, that we might not live if I did not have this baby immediately. That was the last thing I heard before I woke up to my brand-new, healthy son.

Crew was born one month after my nineteenth birthday. It took me some time to heal from the complications of his birth, and while I was healing, I began to notice that my child did not seem to react like other children. When I tried to cuddle and embrace him, he stiffened and pulled away. He cried excessively and often held his breath until he turned blue. His energy was closed, hard, and rigid. I noticed that on the days when I was angry and cried all day long, so did he. I was disconnected from my Spirit at this time in my life, so I brushed this awareness off.

Looking back, if I had only invoked the energy of Archangel Zadkiel, my life would have been different. But I wasn't ready, and the toxic life that I had created for myself continued. My boyfriend and I fought all the time. We lived in a small shack that he had built adjacent to his mom's garage. We had no heat or air conditioning, no bed, and oftentimes no working toilet or shower. Even though I was now working three part-time jobs, I had to apply for welfare so that I could cover basic living expenses. Not only was it embarrassing to live this way, but it made me more angry. My own self-judgment which caused me to refuse to ask for help fueled even more anger. We were on welfare, while my boyfriend was drinking and smoking away what little income he brought in. This cycle went on for nearly two years before I gathered up the strength to move out and then move out of state.

Although I removed myself from that unhealthy environment, as my son got older, he became even more defiant and difficult. He was angry and often full of rage. He was also very sensitive and emotional, so his anger fueled mine and vice versa. We both felt out of control. I would hold him down during time outs, and he would bite, hit, kick, and throw things at me. Thank goodness I never spanked him, for I was afraid if I started, I would never stop. My anger was his anger, and, all along, he was just trying to escape from what was never his. The anger, sadness, and pain that lived inside me were mirrored every time I looked into my son's eyes.

One weekend when Crew was ten years old, he went to stay at my mom's house. I was grateful for the quiet moments I had to myself and looked forward to this time of renewal. I received a phone call from my mom. She was upset, frightened, and concerned that Crew might hurt her or one of us when he was angry. When I heard those words, ten years of emotions came pouring out. I started defending myself and Crew, and assured her that I was doing everything I could possibly do, and had been for years, but nothing had worked. She was convinced that one day he was going to end up in jail if I did not do something. As I listened to her, tears fell from my eyes as the pain of her words went straight to my heart. I told her I would never let that happen to my son, and I never wanted to hear the word "prison" again. I couldn't take it any longer. I had to figure something else out, and I was going to leave no stone unturned. I would do whatever I needed to do—and finally I did.

Something inside me "woke up," and I asked for help for the first time—from the Universe, my Spirit Guides, and my Angels. I asked for guidance and a sign or message that would tell me what to do. I prayed, cried, screamed, yelled, and finally let go. I realized that I had been trying to fix my life all on my own and had forgotten about my spiritual support team. As I sat with that awareness, I was shocked. I had called on my Angels in so many other areas of my life—why did I forget to ask for help in my greatest challenge? I didn't ask because I didn't feel that I deserved it. I had created this terrible situation, this difficult and challenging child; therefore, I didn't deserve help—period!

So I began with forgiveness, and I invoked the powerful energy of Archangel Zadkiel. I asked him to guide and support me in finding forgiveness for myself so I could heal from within. As soon as I spoke the words, I felt immediate relief in my heart. Over time, I noticed subtle changes in my son's behavior. Archangel Zadkiel helped me find compassion for myself and my situation. Archangel Zadkiel gave me strength and courage to break down the walls and begin to love myself. Little by little, I got better. I realized that as much as I tried to fight it, my son came here to be my teacher. As soon as I started forgiving myself and loving myself through the guilt, pain, and anger, my son stopped being my mirror. The energy shifted, and we both moved forward in harmony instead of resistance.

Oftentimes, it is our children who are our greatest teachers. It isn't always easy to recognize this when you are in the middle of an experience. I was the mom, yet being a parent didn't automatically make me a teacher. I took responsibility for my creation. I allowed it, and I accepted the situation. However, my baby boy did not have that choice. I was carrying a lot of shame and guilt over the choices that I'd made, but throughout the process of forgiving myself and my actions, I felt Archangel Zadkiel's supportive energy.

I moved through layers of healing. Forgiving myself, at times, felt nearly impossible. It was a lot of work. Forgiveness isn't easy. I had to come to peace with all the doctors, medication, therapists, and denial. My son went through hell—to heal me. Some days I felt grateful, other days, sad. When I found myself slipping back, I reconnected with the violet ray of Archangel Zadkiel. I imagined the violet energy swirling around in my heart space, and I asked him to soften my heart so that I could forgive the pain and sadness I had created in my life and in my son's life. I asked him to show me the bigger picture, the value, and the purpose in this entire experience. The healthier I became, the better my son got. Crew continues to be my greatest teacher, but now we both learn through love. For in my process of forgiveness, I found an unconditional love for myself.

VALUE OF THE EXPERIENCE: Only by forgiving and healing yourself will you find the energy shift between yourself and others. True forgiveness transforms you when you find the value in each experience.

Healing Your Heart: A Nine-Step Archangel Process

Stone walls do not a prison make,
Nor iron bars a cage;
Minds innocent of quiet take
That for an hermitage;
If I have freedom in my love
And in my soul am free,
Angels alone that soar above
Enjoy such liberty.

—Richard Lovelace

In healing my own heart, I've found that there's an evolutionary process that occurs as I move from awareness to appreciation. I've broken this process down into nine steps so that you can recognize where you are currently and then see where you can move to. I will be using my own life experiences as examples of how you can use these steps to open up, ask for help from the Archangels, and allow healing into your heart. By witnessing my journey from beginning to end, it is my hope that you can take what fits for you, relate it to your own present or past circumstances, and reach a place where true healing is realized. This is my story of self-love and forgiveness.

Step 1: Awareness

Awareness is the state or ability to perceive, to feel, or to be conscious. Typically you become aware of a challenge, an illness, an emotion, or a desire. You can also have self-awareness. Self-awareness is the ability to perceive one's own existence, traits, feelings, and behaviors. You become aware of your own personality or individuality.

DESCRIPTION: Becoming aware is usually the simplest step. Awareness typically comes through pain as we literally become "aware" of the pain. This pain can be physical, mental, emotional, or spiritual. The pain can be caused by a variety of different things, such as unhealthy relationships, illness or disease, unresolved emotions, lack of boundaries, death, dissatisfaction—the list goes on and on. Pain, on some level, is usually what wakes us up into awareness.

The pain can be something we've had in our lives for a long time; therefore, we don't even recognize it or are in denial of it. Our friends and family often help us become aware of the pain by pointing out areas in our lives that are working and/or not working. Sometimes their approach is loving, and sometimes it is not. If you feel defensive, then a defensive response is the validation that what they are saying may have some truth behind it. Sometimes those around us and outside us can see more clearly than we can.

You can invoke Archangel Uriel for clarity and understanding in situations like this. Archangel Uriel's energy will guide you from a place of love and help you to see what is going on around you and within you. His presence helps you to acknowledge that you have an issue that needs your attention. Angels often speak through the people in our lives. Angels are the conduits that guide us, sight unseen, into an awareness that healing is available. As we acknowledge the message, and become aware, we take the first step toward healing. In this step, you don't need to know "what to do" or "how to do it," you simply become aware of the fact that there is something to do.

PERSONAL EXPERIENCE: My awareness began in August 1989. I had just turned eighteen years old and was working full time, supporting my musician boyfriend, John. We had recently moved in together. I was on the outs with my parents, more so my dad, because he did not approve of me dating John. Instead of fighting all the time, I chose to move out. Initially, I felt proud of myself and was happy to finally be doing what I wanted to do. I was so tired of being told what I could and could not do, and the judgment and criticism of my choices was getting old. I was relieved to be away from the drama.

My dad had recently had an affair, and I was still pretty angry at him. Actually, I was angry at both of my parents. I could not understand why my mom would choose to stay with my dad after she found out he'd had an affair. I knew that she wanted to leave, and she even tried, but she just couldn't do it. She loved him too much. I would soon come to my own understanding and experience of how that codependency can run your life, but right then, I was just happy to be out of their home and making my own life decisions.

My boyfriend, his mom Delores, and I were living in a rundown house, half a mile off a dirt road. This was a completely different lifestyle from the $350,000 house I had just moved away from. But I was still happy, because in my leaving, I got to make a choice. For a while, things went well. This was my first real relationship, and I soaked up the feeling of being wanted and needed.

When we had first started dating, we had fun and partied quite a bit on the weekends. Once I was living with him, I began to notice that perhaps he was drinking too much. Drinking every day seemed a bit much to me, but I passed it off, and on the weekends, when I wasn't working, I joined in. That was my way of dealing with it. If you can't beat them, join them. That lasted a few months.

There was one particular weekend when we had been out partying. After we came home, I got really sick. That had never happened to me before, so I "knew" something wasn't right, but I ignored it. This sickness lasted for two weeks, and I noticed that it was worse in the mornings. I soon realized that I had missed my period, but because I was on birth control, I just figured I was late. Another week passed, and I decided to do a pregnancy test. I got one of those "do it yourself" kits because I did not want anyone to know. The test came back positive, and I sobbed. I was scared to tell anyone, so I hid the test in the trunk of my car, hoping the pregnancy might just "go away." I was now *aware* that I had a problem. A big, *big* problem!

Step 2: Looking Within

You have to have a willingness to look within and ask for help. Unfortunately, many of us look outside ourselves for answers to our questions. The key is to get in touch with the inner you and acknowledge the intuitive power that you have. Oftentimes, decisions are based from the ego and not the Spirit. By looking within, the path becomes clear and uncluttered.

DESCRIPTION: Once you have an awareness of a situation, it is time to step out of judgment and your ego and look within. You have to be willing to see from your heart. Depending on the situation, this can be very challenging. Questions may come up, such as "How did I get here? What did I do to deserve this? Why me? What do I need to do now? How will I ever move forward?" Sometimes the victim energy takes over, and we begin to blame others or spend hours trapped in our own negative self-talk. This is not the time to beat yourself up or listen to the voices of others. This is really an opportunity to listen within, to travel into that deepest part of your inner knowing and get an honest assessment of where you are and how you got there.

It's a great time to ask your Angels and guides to help you stay focused on the answers within and not let your mind run away with the fear of what everyone, including you, might think. Take an accurate, unbiased look at your situation with a loving and supportive heart. When you ask with an open heart, your intuitive guidance speaks up. Call on Archangel Raphael to help you have the spiritual insight to see what is truly going on within you. Invoking Raphael's energy as a source of support, clear sight, and healing is an amazing gift. His energy and insight will help you to see how the situation manifested; with this knowledge, you will then be prepared to move forward.

PERSONAL EXPERIENCE: After my pregnancy test came back positive, it was time to look within. I initially fell into the victim mentality and questioned everything. How did I get pregnant in the first place? Don't get me wrong; I knew "how" I got pregnant, but I was on birth control and couldn't understand how "the pill" had failed me. I was always the smart one. I had never wanted children. My plan was to go to school and make something of my life. Although I had dropped out of high school at age fifteen, I still managed to graduate two and a half years early at age sixteen by taking an equivalency test. So I had plans, big plans. Then, in one moment's time, my plans started to crumble. How could this happen to me? My life was ruined, and I felt like I had no choice for a future.

Looking within was very painful. I didn't find any answers, and I didn't trust what Spirit was telling me. All I heard was: "Everything happens for a reason," and I certainly didn't believe that now. Before this experience, I would have said yes, I do believe that everything happens for a reason. But in this particular situation, I was struggling to find a reason.

I was scared for myself and terrified of others' opinions. I knew there would be a lot of "talk" among my friends, family, and extended family. In Salt Lake City, Utah, the thought of a pregnant teenager was just unacceptable. I knew I would be judged and looked down upon. I didn't think the religious judgment would bother me, since I had distanced myself from that part of my upbringing; but the truth is, it did bother me—a lot. I was tired of always being different and feeling like an outcast. I just wanted to be "normal." But I wasn't. I was different, and I knew that.

So I had no other choice but to go back within and be open to the guidance I received. Once I moved through the despair and sat quietly, I realized that I did have a choice. I could choose to not have this baby. I could choose to fix this mistake by having an abortion. It would be *my* choice, and no one would ever need to know.

Step 3: Choice

Choice simply means the act of choosing. You always have a choice to react or act. The kind of life you have is the life you choose. In this process, choice is the foundation of change. Sometimes you perceive your choice as a right choice or a wrong choice; but my point is, you still have a choice.

DESCRIPTION: When it comes to making a choice, regardless of what area of your life it is in, it can feel like there is a right choice and a wrong choice. You can postpone making a choice, which is actually choosing not to choose, for fear of making the "wrong choice." Not choosing is still a choice. When you get to the third step in the process, invite Archangel Gabriel to surround you and support you. His loving guidance will help you to see clearly that, first and foremost, there is no "right" or "wrong." In right and wrong, there is judgment. In truth, you are making the best choice you can with the information and knowledge you have at any particular time.

There is often judgment wrapped around "choice," and if we can release that judgment, be open, and ask for guidance from the Archangels, then many options will become available. You can't skip life lessons, no matter how connected or evolved you believe you are. Many times it is in the choice that we gain our greatest awareness of who we are.

When you are faced with a choice, ask Archangel Gabriel to surround you, and listen to the guidance you receive. The guidance may or may not be subtle. It can come in the form of a sudden feeling, a suggestion from a friend, in song lyrics that speak to your heart, or through a knowingness that manifests immediately. These are just some examples of ways in which Archangel Gabriel works in our lives. The important thing to be conscious of is that you need to love yourself enough to choose, for in the act of choosing, you move forward. Even if you move into something you do not want, you will gain clarity through that experience to help you make different and better choices. You will find that, as you invoke the Archangels for guidance, moving through experiences will become easier, and your choices will ultimately come from within you instead of from outside yourself. When we make choices based on what's "within," then we begin to live an authentic life.

PERSONAL EXPERIENCE: I made a choice. I sat with it, looked at it, and when I went within, I felt empty, alone, afraid, and sad. But I still made a choice to have an abortion. I heard the message, "Everything happens for a reason," and I still could not find a reason other than this was meant to ruin my life. I was not even cut out to be a mom, and when I toyed with the idea, it sent me into a panic. I didn't know the first thing about raising a child, for heaven's sake. I had barely even baby-sat. I also realized that my boyfriend was in no shape to become a parent. He spent many of his days and nights drinking, so if I were to keep this child, I would have to go it alone. In my mind, this was not an option.

I arrived at the pregnancy center, and from the moment I met the staff, I felt the guilt. Each conversation I had focused on what would happen to the baby and my body if I had an abortion. Pictures of each stage of the embryo lined the walls as they escorted me to a movie about the abortion process. I felt the judgment as I passed a lady in the hallway. The dialog in my head was "How can you murder an innocent life?"

Hours before, my choice had been clear, but now I wasn't so sure. I was overwhelmed with emotion and started to cry. My heart was telling me that I could not go through with the abortion. Hours ago, my head had told me I could not raise a child. But in this moment, my heart told me I could. I believe the Angels guided me to this experience so that I could move past the emptiness, loneliness, and fear and get into my heart and make the choice from that space.

I chose to keep my child. I told my boyfriend that I had changed my mind and that I was keeping the baby. He knew I had made up my mind by the look of certainty on my face. With a sense of anxiety and apprehension, he gave me a hug and said, "I guess we are going to have a baby then," and we left the pregnancy center as soon-to-be parents.

As I left the building, I was terrified. I didn't know what I was stepping into. Motherhood, and worse yet, single motherhood, was all I could focus on. I recognized that my entire life was about to change. But I did believe everything happens for a reason; and if that is true, then this had to be a part of the everything. In the deepest part of my knowing, I had made this choice from my heart space, so I knew there would be gifts along the way. There had to be. I never could have imagined how the next twenty-one years would unfold.

Step 4: Commitment

The most important single factor in an individual's success is commitment. Commitment ignites action. To commit means to devote yourself to a purpose or cause.

DESCRIPTION: When you make a commitment to yourself, it can be easy to break. We break these promises because we can. Often there are no external consequences, as you are the only one you have to answer to. If you made a commitment to exercise, eat healthily, watch less TV, read more, or walk the dog nightly, who would know if you didn't keep the promise? It's like a secret game we play with ourselves; we like to keep it quiet in case we decide not to follow through. We like to have an "out." Ultimately, though, you will begin to feel guilty for breaking your promises to yourself. Guilt is the emotional manifestation of broken commitments.

Conversely, we tend to worry more about breaking commitments to someone else. As a society, we tend to put more value on others' perceptions than we do on our own. I remember being taught that what others think of you is more important than what you think of yourself. This was what many of us were taught. Most of the time, the lesson is unintentional. However, we ultimately learn to put others before ourselves. It is an old-school belief. The truth of the matter is, you are most important. What you think about yourself is what creates you and the life you are living!

When you commit to making changes, and you become consciously aware of what you desire, you begin to manifest the support around you for the change to occur. This happens in the physical as well as the spiritual realm. Asking for the guidance and support of Archangel Michael is an important step in maintaining your commitments. Michael helps us with clarity. Invoking his energy to support you as you move forward in your commitment will lighten your load and allow you to receive the support you desire and deserve.

There will be days when you have less energy to keep your commitments. You may even question your choices. This is normal. It is important to be gentle with yourself and love yourself through this time. It will pass. This is not a time for action. If you are feeling unclear, ask Archangel Michael for guidance and wait to make any decisions until you feel the vibration of love and clarity sweep over you.

PERSONAL EXPERIENCE: Once I had made the choice to have my baby, I felt some relief. As painful and challenging as making the choice was, I could now move forward to the next step of commitment. I made a commitment to myself and my unborn baby that no matter what happened, together we would ride it out. I made a commitment to motherhood and everything that comes with it. I committed, even though I didn't know who would support me, what I would do, or where I would live. Luckily for me, I had no idea what was to come in the next few months, or I might have made another choice. However, once I'd made this commitment to myself,

I knew it was for my highest good and that I couldn't back out. I'd made a vow, and I was keeping it.

I kept my commitment by first telling my parents that I was pregnant and that I had made the choice to keep the baby. They were shocked and concerned, but accepting. My parents became very supportive and protective of me. Without their love and support, I wouldn't have made it. I continued to affirm my commitment as I told more and more people. I was feeling good about holding my power and standing in my truth. I knew I had made the best decision for myself, whether others understood it or not.

As you know, four months into my pregnancy, I became very ill. I found my commitment being challenged when I had to make the choice to move back home with my parents. It was hard to do, but I was very sick and needed someone to care for me—I had committed to this baby. I listened to the doctors and went on complete bed rest for the last five months of the pregnancy. I had also committed to seeing the doctor every day, either for blood work and a urine test or for ultrasounds and "fetal non-stress tests." These visits were the only times I was allowed to be upright, aside from using the bathroom. I maintained this commitment to avoid being hospitalized. With the help of my parents, who drove me back and forth every day, I did it.

Some days were challenging, and I wanted to back out. I couldn't stand it anymore. Living with my parents was difficult on everyone. They were truly wonderful and helpful, but I felt like a child again. My mom is a caretaker by nature. All of my needs were taken care of, moment by moment, but at times I found it all to be just too much. I later understood that it was my lack of worthiness that was again rearing its ugly head. I was caught between my commitment to myself and my baby, and my misery—both physical and emotional. But somehow I found a way. I found a way to keep that commitment, even when I questioned it.

The first time I went into labor, I was in tremendous pain. I was not given any pain medication because I was only dilated to half a centimeter after twenty-eight hours. You can be sure I wanted to back out of my commitment then! I wanted to go home and make another choice—and I was given that exact option. The doctors sent me home instead of letting the labor progress. And with that, I found that some commitments you cannot back out of, so I continued to move forward. Nine days later, after an extremely difficult labor, stroke, and emergency Caesarean section, my son was born. It was now time to maintain the commitment that I'd made to my son. I couldn't be just any mom, I had to be the best mom I could be to him.

My best was different on different days. In the beginning, it was really hard. It was all new. I didn't know how to take care of a baby. I felt as if we were teaching each other. This tiny little person was teaching me how to be a mom. As he grew, I recognized that I had committed to giving him the best life I could. I knew that Archangel Michael would guide me and help me maintain my commitment. Archangel Michael never wavered from his assurance that this was all happening for a reason, and I had to believe that there was something better to look forward to. I just hoped it would get easier sooner, rather than later.

Step 5: Responsibility

Responsibility means accepting that you and you alone are accountable for your life. There is no one to blame. Being responsible comes with the realization that you are where you are because of your own conduct, beliefs, and behavior. Your choices have created the experiences you are living right now. The good news is that you are responsible for your life. The bad news is that you are responsible for your life.

DESCRIPTION: Responsibility plays a key role in healing your heart. When you take responsibility for your life—your actions, beliefs, and experiences—you are halfway through the healing process. Often, when people think of responsibility, there is a feeling of guilt or a perception of something being wrong. Responsibility simply means to "own" your power. It means that you are willing to recognize that *you* are the creator of your life and that your thoughts, words, and actions manifest events and experiences in your life. You begin to see that you are not a victim of others but a powerful creator of your life.

When we take responsibility, we learn our own power. We do not give it away by blaming others. Responsibility means you are willing to release the need to project your anger and frustration onto others, because you know that, ultimately, you attract experiences into your life for a reason.

Invoking Archangel Jophiel, the Angel of beauty, is a first step in beginning to accept responsibility in your life. His energy will help you to see the beauty around you. He will help you recognize the gifts that are in your life at this exact moment. As you begin to see more beauty around you, your thoughts begin to change in a positive direction. When you see yourself through the eyes of beauty, you begin to manifest more beauty in your life. You will begin to see yourself as the powerful creator you are without fear, blame, or guilt. When you put responsibility in someone else's hands, you also hand over your power to them, and you can feel powerless. But when you take responsibility, you have the power; then, and only then, can you heal anything.

Personal Experience: If being the best mom I could be to my son Crew was my commitment, I realized that the environment that we were living in was my responsibility. It was easy to blame his father, John, for everything, but I had to move from blame to responsibility. I wanted something different for myself and my son. I was a smart girl, and the way I was living was no longer acceptable to me. I didn't know how to make these changes by myself. I was scared to do it alone. My parents had recently moved from California to Arizona, so I was completely on my own. The fighting, the shack we were living in, the alcohol, the fear of the lack of money, the fear of *everything*—it all took a toll on me. I knew it was my responsibility to do something, but what could I do? I was on welfare, for heaven's sake, and I had nothing. I had about three hundred dollars to my name, and that was it. Part of me felt as if I deserved this life. I created it, and I needed to accept my fate. But a little voice came back and reminded me that "everything happens for a reason."

There are moments in our lives that we never forget. The day I spoke with Dr. Laura Schlesinger on the phone was one of those moments for me. A light bulb moment, one that changed my life forever. It was one o'clock on Easter morning, and I was home alone with Crew because John had decided to stay out all night with his buddies. I could tell he had been drinking, and I was disappointed that he did not want to come home to spend Easter with his family. Actually "disappointed" is not the word—I was pissed. I turned on the radio to distract myself from my feelings and tuned into a radio talk show with Dr. Laura Schlesinger. I had never heard of her before, so I was curious and began to listen.

She invited people to call in with any questions. I thought to myself, boy do I have questions. I decided to call and got right on the air. I started giving her all the details of my life. I was a teenage mom, living in a shack with a boyfriend who would rather stay out drinking than come home for Easter. I asked her what I should do about him. Before I could even finish my sentence, she interrupted me by saying, "Listen, Sunny, there are two kinds of men in this world. There are the kinds of men that want families, and there are the kinds of men that don't. It sounds to me like you have one that doesn't!" And with that message, she hung up.

I was furious. I couldn't believe that she had spoken to me that way. She wasn't even interested in hearing the rest of my story. I felt worthless, as usual. I cried myself to sleep that night, once again.

Over the next two days, her message played over and over in my head. Something inside me knew she was right, although she could have been a little more gentle in her delivery! But the point was she was right. So, I packed up my car with all of my belongings and left. My son was fifteen months old when I finally took complete responsibility for the environment we were living in. This step truly changed the direction of our lives, and it allowed me to give my son the best possible life I could—even if I was a single, teenaged parent. Everything happens for a reason!

Step 6: Action

Action is the state or process of acting or doing something to achieve a purpose. In this step, you take action, and you invoke the healing energy of the Archangels.

DESCRIPTION: Once you have made a commitment and taken responsibility for your life and choices, it is time to take action. You begin by looking at the "reason" you take an action. Are you acting because you are afraid, or is your action heart based? If you act out of fear, you will only attract more fear. This is an example of forced action: taking action because you feel as if you need to. This type of action is often ego based and can manifest as "digging a deeper hole." However, if you take action from a vibration of willingness and openness, then this will attract loving experiences and helpers along the way. This is called inspired action: taking action that is guided by Spirit. This more Spirit-based approach can manifest as "effortless and gentle direction."

Asking the Archangels to guide you to inspired action will help move you away from your head toward your heart. Taking action from your heart will move you forward, not sideways. When you are inspired (in-Spirit), you are guided from the Spirit world. When you allow the Archangels to guide you, in the divine right time and space, they will always guide you to the best possible next step. Allowing them to be of service to you makes this action step straightforward and simple.

PERSONAL EXPERIENCE: Once I took responsibility, I knew it was time to take action. I could no longer look the other way, feel sorry for myself, or hide in blame. After I'd heard Dr. Laura's message, I knew I needed to take action from a place of trust. I prayed for help. I asked anyone and everyone who would listen—God, the Angels, my guides and helpers—to guide me to a place where my son and I would be safe and comfortable.

The day I moved out, John was at a friend's house, so he didn't know I was leaving. I had taken as many of my belongings as would fit in my car. The first thing I did was buy a newspaper, so that I could look for places to rent. I was hoping to find an ad for a roommate or perhaps a house that was renting out a room. I could not afford to lease an apartment, as that was too expensive, and I didn't have any credit or a cosigner.

I was scared. What if the people I encountered were crazy? What if I put our safety at risk? But as quickly as these fears came up, they were dismissed by my heavenly protector's loving vibration. I *knew* that we would be okay. I knew that the Angels would guide me to the right place at the right time. So, with newspaper in hand, we went searching for our new home.

I circled five ads that looked like they might work for me. When I called the first two places, they asked if I had children. I said I had a fifteen-month-old child, and they immediately declined. I was now left with three options. I met with two of the landlords, and I knew right away that it wasn't going to work. One that seemed quite promising had several cats, which I was allergic to, so that was out. The other place was filthier than the shack I had just moved out of. My goal was to move forward, not sideways. So I had one more house to visit, and it was nearly five o'clock on a Friday evening. The house I was interested in was located in the city of Lake Elsinore. As I drove through the neighborhood, the scenery was a paradise compared to where I had been living. The yards were neatly groomed, and the houses were beautiful. It almost seemed too good to be true. I pulled up to the advertised house and went to the door. I had Crew on my hip and was eager to speak with the landlord. I knocked and a lady answered. I told her why I was there, and she pointed out to me that the ad said no kids. With tears streaming down my face, I told her that this was the only house I had left on my list. I had to find a place to live, and I had nowhere to go if she said no. I begged her for a chance and convinced her that I could be a helpful hand and that I would respect her space. Although her energy felt like she wanted to say no, her lips said, "Okay. I will give you one month. I am a single parent too, and I know what that is like." I was so grateful. I gave her the three hundred dollars that I had started saving even before Crew was born. I knew that someday I would need the money to move out, and that someday was today. I emptied the car with the help of a friend, and Crew and I moved in that very day.

A couple of days later, John finally realized that Crew and I had left the house. He had just come home after the weekend to find that our stuff was gone. He called me up and didn't understand why I had left. I had told him numerous times that I was going to leave if things didn't change. I tried to explain to him how unhealthy our relationship was. He was always drinking, I was codependent, and I was through being in that type of relationship. It wasn't healthy for us, and it certainly wasn't healthy for Crew. He said he would change, do better, and quit drinking. As we talked, I felt my resolve slipping away. I could feel myself taking on his emotions and sadness. It began to take me over, too. He begged me to give him another chance, and, without much thought, I did. However, this time, I had conditions.

The first condition was that I would stay living at my own place, and he could come and visit Crew and me there. The second condition was that he was not allowed to drink around us, and when he was with his friends, he could only drink up to a six-pack. The third condition was that by the New Year of 1992, he had to quit drinking completely. He agreed, and he honored this agreement for a couple of weeks.

I was excited because I felt like maybe he was turning over a new leaf. I thought that maybe, just maybe, we could make this work and that we would become a real family. But as time went on and parties or gigs or band practice came up, he would disregard our agreement and step back into his comfort zone, which was to drink heavily. Over the next five months, this cycle repeated, and we would argue until I cried. Many nights, I'd lie awake thinking, if he just loved me enough or just loved Crew enough, he would quit. But he didn't. It was at this time that I went back to the Al-Anon meetings that I had attended early in my pregnancy. I was still searching for answers on how I could help him.

As time progressed, I realized that he was not going to be the person I wanted him to be or the dad I wanted for my son. I loved him, but I soon realized that the love I had for him was coming from a place of lack within myself. I was addicted to the chaos and drama that our relationship provided, and I finally refused to keep the cycle going. On December 27, 1991, I made the decision to leave— really leave. My parents were coming to town for my uncle's funeral, and when I found that out, I asked them if they'd be willing to bring the truck to my house. I was ready. I explained that I was leaving John for good. They were very supportive and came to help me pack up my belongings to move back to Arizona with them.

Walking away from a life that had created so much contrast for me was one of the hardest things I've done. The day I took my son literally out of his father's hands is a day I will never forget. John would not let either of us go, and I had to pull Crew from John's arms. I ran to the car sobbing. I got Crew into the car seat as quickly as I could and drove away. I never looked back. I was on our way to our new home in Tucson, Arizona. I cried most of the eight-hour drive and had plenty of time to think in between the tears. For the majority of our three-year relationship, I had cried. I decided then and there that I would not enter into another relationship where I cried more than I laughed—and I never did. That night, I took my power back, power that I had given away, and I finally understood that John had provided a valuable lesson in my life. He had come to teach me to love myself. Everything happens for a reason.

Step 7: Releasing and Replenishing

Releasing is often defined as an emotional purging. Our emotions, thoughts, and beliefs are contained in our bodies, so learning to release these will help you achieve more peace, happiness, and emotional well-being. Replenishing simply means to fill back up or make complete again. Emotional purging often leaves empty spaces within—and since nature abhors a vacuum, you must fill yourself back up.

DESCRIPTION: Releasing is simply letting go—letting go of guilt, shame, pain, beliefs, and old energy. To release is to surrender to something greater, to forgive, and to move forward in love. When releasing the old and stepping into the new, you want to remember that what you release needs to be replaced with a higher vibrational feeling, thought, or belief. In other words, as we let go, we need to fill up. If we do not do the two together, we run the risk of attracting the same type of energy that we wish to release, only in a new and different form. We unconsciously allow a similar vibration into our space; it is simply masked as something new. When we release, we *must* replenish to bring in the newer, higher vibrations.

There are many ways to release the energy that is holding you back from living the life you desire. First and foremost, invoke Archangel Zadkiel's energy of mercy and benevolence. His energy will help you to heal your own emotions and release anything that no longer serves you. You can also visualize the violet forgiving energy of Archangel Zadkiel surrounding you. Visualize this violet energy absorbing all of the negativity and pain that you have carried in your mind and body. Know that you can let it go; it has served you well, but it is now time to be released.

There are many ways to release emotion. Journaling is a great tool for releasing anger and shame. I often advise my clients to burn the pages when they are done so as to transmute the old energy and raise its vibration. You can also scream, yell, and beat the crap out of pillows, punching bags, or your bed. (No people, please!) You can affirm: "I am willing to release _____."

An important thing to remember is that when you begin to release, you will most likely feel a pull—a strong pull—toward that which you just released. You may unconsciously step in the direction of attracting more of it into your life. This is why sometimes it seems as though once we get committed and are willing to release, things get harder. It isn't that it is getting harder, but we are more aware of that negative attraction or pull. That is where replenishing comes in. This is why it is equally important to replenish yourself with loving energy. I call in Archangel Chamuel to help with this. I invoke his unconditional loving energy and visualize the color pink as I breathe in. His loving energy washes away the pain, sadness, and fear. You can actually feel and witness his energy shifting your vibration. It fills you up, on a cellular level, with a love that you have not previously allowed to enter into the barren places of your body. Allow yourself to receive this unconditional love and know that with this positive loving energy, you can begin to create an amazing life of love and light.

PERSONAL EXPERIENCE: Now that I was living in Tucson, Arizona, for the first time in a long time, I felt like I could start over again. I had a lot of fears about being in a relationship. My old memory tapes continued to play every once in a while, and I would hear the words in my head that I had been told so many times before: "You are not fun anymore. Who's

going to want someone like you? You're a stick in the mud."
I wondered if anyone would really want to date someone my
age, especially somebody who already had a child. I was glad
that my Angels were around to counteract my negative self-
talk. As soon as I started, they would say things such as, "You
have a lot to offer. You are fun. You deserve someone who
appreciates your maturity and commitment to your son."
Most importantly, "You have done well." Every time I heard
these whispers in my ear, I felt better, and I released just a
little more of that self-judgment.

Even though I was missing the presence of a partner,
a mate, a companion, I realized that I needed to do some
healing, releasing, and refilling before I could think about
another relationship. I decided to take a year off from dating
and focus solely on me and my son. I had become too serious,
as I equated being responsible with being serious. I decided
to have some fun and lighten up a little. I realized that I was
feeling empty, disconnected from life, and I needed to learn
who I was. I was twenty years old, and it was time for me to
figure out who Sunny was. I wasn't just a mother, or a daughter, or a sister. I was Sunny, and I needed to work on who she
was and what she wanted.

To begin my search, I went back to *You Can Heal Your
Life* and started doing affirmations, mirror work, and, most
importantly, forgiveness work. I started going out to dance
clubs, and I loved this. It provided a nice escape from my son
who was smack in the middle of the Terrible Twos.

So began the road to forgiveness and a search for the tools
that I could use to love and accept myself. I carried a ton of
guilt and shame for the experiences I had allowed my son to

live through. The guilt had begun the moment he was conceived and continued for many years. I was carrying a lot of anger toward many people, and I knew it was time to begin to release that, as well. I took some steps forward, but some days I would find myself right smack dab back in the anger and guilt again. I tried to be gentle with my healing process as I took two steps forward and sometimes five steps back. In the midst of releasing my anger, I soon realized what I really needed to release was fear. Fear manifests in many forms, and for me, it was guilt, shame, anger, frustration, and loss of control. These were the *big five* for me.

I spent days, then weeks, then months releasing. With all this letting go, I was feeling lighter but emptier. I knew I needed to learn some ways to fill up what I was releasing so that I would not unconsciously manifest the negativity again. I asked for help from the Spirit world. I don't recall that I asked any particular Archangel—I just asked! I began each day with the affirmation: "I am open and receptive to all that is good." This would help me set an intention for the day and remind me to stay open to the good, not to push it away (which was something I had done unconsciously in the past).

Outside of parenthood, I was beginning to feel better about myself. I was starting to gather some "tools" to support myself. My mom was a great help, as she had encouraged me to read some of her self-help books. They assisted me to find my light and self-esteem. I even got back into journaling. I wrote poetry and studied numerology and spirituality once again. I was beginning to feel better by releasing and replenishing.

It was time to open up my heart again to find a mate, but I was still frightened. I had spent the last year taking baby steps to learn how to love myself again. I was afraid to open up, yet I knew it was time. I knew it intuitively. So, because I wanted to move into my fear while taking baby steps, I decided to open up on paper first, instead of affirming it aloud. It seemed less scary that way.

I created a list of the "Perfect Partner Qualities." I came up with about forty qualities that I really wanted in a partner and then tucked the list away in my journal. I didn't want anyone to see it, as it felt kind of silly. But I figured it couldn't hurt, and maybe, just maybe, I'd get lucky. It also felt good to have my desires on paper, out of my head and in the physical. It seemed to make them more "real" for me, or at least more possible. I said a little prayer in the hopes that one day, I would be able to attract a man with all of the qualities that I wanted. I even took a moment to imagine and feel what it would be like to have someone who was kind and gentle and a family man—my top three qualities.

On a Wednesday night, February 3, 1993, my life changed again—and, finally, it was for the better. I met Brett John-ston, the man on my list. I knew within a few hours of meeting him that he was "the guy." As I got to know him, I realized that he had every quality I had listed, with two exceptions (which were negotiable anyway). I knew, as we dated, that I had finally released the patterns of my past relationships. I knew it because I could feel the change within me. I felt full. I felt happy. I felt excited about my future and my life. I felt I was actually being who I really was, and I was okay. I knew that with this man's help, I would continue to learn to love and forgive myself. His love allowed me to see myself through different eyes. He showed me what unconditional love meant when he embraced Crew and me exactly the way we were. We became a family almost immediately and were married nine months later at the top of Merry-Go-Round Rock in Sedona, Arizona.

Step 8: Maintenance

In this case, maintenance means to maintain and protect your own energy and vibration. It is important to protect your energy. If you don't do this, you risk breaking down your own energy resources at all levels: physical, emotional, mental, and spiritual.

DESCRIPTION: Maintaining and protecting your own energy and vibration is very important in healing the heart. Many people live in a world where they absorb the negative thoughts and feelings of both living and deceased energies. At times, this energy can feel overwhelming and scary; therefore, people start to live in fear of their own emotions.

Throughout this section, I will use the words "protect" and "maintain" interchangeably. The word protection is perceived as the safeguarding of somebody or something; the act of preventing somebody or something from being harmed or damaged; or the state of being kept safe. However, when I use the word protection, I mean maintaining your own energy, being mindful of your energy and how you choose to absorb or take on the energy of others around you. Protection means to witness rather than absorb. Witnessing may feel like you are detaching from someone or some situation, but detachment does not mean you don't care. Detachment means you are willing to let go of your expectations of what someone else *should* feel or not feel.

Energy shifts and moves constantly throughout the day. It can shift as your mood changes, as you interact with others, or as a result of your thoughts. You live in a constantly changing energy field, yet how often do you think of keeping your energy field clear and clean? Whose energy are you tapped in to? How often do you feel tired after hanging up the phone or grabbing a bite to eat with a friend? Do you avoid the lunchroom because the co-worker who often complains eats at the same time as you do? My point is, it is critical to protect your energy from the minute you get up in the morning—and if you feel it necessary, again several times throughout the day. I promise you, you will feel a greater sense of freedom as you begin to unplug and disconnect from all the energies around you!

There are several ways that you can protect your energy. They include:

- the White Light Prayer (see appendix)

- the visualization of "The Blue Bubble" (see appendix)

- invoking Archangel Michael and the Angels to protect your energy (see appendix)

- becoming aware of your feelings and discerning if they are your own; and if not, releasing them

- physical tools, such as essential oils, smudging, sprays, and crystals

PERSONAL EXPERIENCE: As a teenager, I was sixty pounds overweight and very insecure. I didn't understand at the time that I was carrying the extra weight because I was so sensitive to the energies around me. I found protection in the extra weight; I "used" it so that I did not have to feel. It was my protection mechanism, but I utilized it without being conscious of how at the time. Food became a source of comfort and a way to separate myself from others. My hypersensitivity made me "different," and food helped mask the feeling that I was not good enough. I was depressed because of the emotions I was feeling from everyone else, and the only thing that would fill me up was food.

After I had ended the relationship with Crew's father John, moved from California to Arizona, and then married Brett, I began to see how much the energy around me affected me. My awareness of my hypersensitivity could not be ignored any longer, and I was finally able to see that when I felt alone, upset, or afraid, I would eat. Eating had become my way of disconnecting from not only my own feelings, but the feelings and emotions of everyone around me. As I began my new life in Phoenix with my new husband, I knew I needed to do something different to maintain my energy.

I finally understood that I was a "feeler," or clairsentient. Feelers absorb the emotional and physical energy of others. I could walk into a room and know if there had been an argument, or I would feel physical pain in my body from a friend who was in distress. I could feel the energy when watching the television news as a pit in my stomach or lump in my throat. As time went on, I had to learn to discern *my* feelings from those of others.

I was a sensitive being, and I needed to learn to walk the world in a different way. I was ready to find that way, so I started to work with the energy of Archangel Michael again. I would call on him at random times during the day, often when I found it most convenient. I would find some relief, but by the end of the evening, I felt like a saturated sponge. It took me several years to realize that working with Archangel Michael was just as important as brushing my teeth and taking a shower. This was my way of "cleaning" my energetic body and protecting my own energy. With that awareness, I committed to working with Archangel Michael every day. Each morning, before I got out of bed, I called in Archangel Michael and imagined a protective sapphire-blue bubble around me. I asked that he surround and protect me. It was that simple.

If I started to feel the emotions of others during the day, I would visualize the sapphire-blue bubble again. And, as I did this, I felt better. For the first time, I felt like I was in control of my own emotional body. I had more energy, and I experienced moments of detachment from the drama of family and friends. I could finally go to the grocery store and come home just as I had left, with only my emotions and not carrying anyone else's emotional baggage. By invoking and working with the energy of Archangel Michael, my life began to change. Because I felt more in control of my emotions, the extra weight that I had carried for protection began to fall off. I was protecting myself energetically, and I no longer needed to do it with food. I had found a way to walk in this world as a sensitive person. I began to "observe" rather than "absorb," and I began to teach about the powerful energy of Archangel Michael. For the last eighteen years, my weight has been very healthy and perfect for my body. Archangel

Michael's blue bubble of protection surrounds me each and every day, and I offer this form of protection to you as well. His protective energy will help you maintain your own.

Step 9: Appreciation

Appreciation is knowing or understanding the value of an experience and is often expressed with feelings of gratitude. In this step, it specifically means to honor an experience with open arms and a healed heart. Oftentimes, once appreciation is experienced, forgiveness follows.

DESCRIPTION: Appreciation is the complete understanding of the meaning and importance of an experience. When we appreciate the people, experiences, energy, and gifts around us, they appreciate—or grow—in value. When we are in a state of appreciation, our ability to expand grows, and the greatness in our lives grows. Our lives become fuller, have more meaning, more love. When we appreciate, we understand why things happened the way they did. Even if it was a painful experience, we see the value of the experience and are no longer pained by it. We actually honor the form of the gift.

In looking at appreciation, we begin to realize that everything that we focus on appreciates (grows). If your focus is on pain, you get more pain. If your focus is on lack of money, you live with not having enough money. If you focus on love, you get more love. As you can see, appreciation is an absolute constant in our lives. You can appreciate consciously or unconsciously; but either way, appreciation is happening all around you.

When you are in appreciation, you feel full, happy, grateful, and positive. You look at the past with gratitude for the knowledge and wisdom you have gained. Sometimes, you can barely remember the painful parts of the past because you have such an innate understanding of the greater purpose. You see the value of the entire experience. If there is forgiveness to be done, and if you are in state of appreciation, the forgiveness has likely already occurred. Forgiveness often goes hand in hand with appreciation.

Invoking the Archangels, each and every one of them, during this time of appreciation, allows them to experience your open heart. You get to experience each one of their vibrations in a space of gratitude instead of a space of need. It can be your way of saying, "Thank you for surrounding me, supporting me, and guiding me through each step of the way."

When we have the feeling of appreciation, we often want to share it with others who may have been a support along the way. We thank them, do kind deeds, and write letters and stories about our blessed life. We even send prayers to the heavens as a form of acknowledgment. The greatest gift of appreciation the Archangels can receive after walking this journey with you, one step at a time, is for your heart to be open, healed, and whole once again.

PERSONAL EXPERIENCE: Once I learned how to maintain my own energy, I was able to keep the feelings of love, joy, and happiness within me for longer periods of time. It seemed that many areas of my life were going really, really well. My husband and I were doing great. He truly was the man of my dreams. Financially, we were doing okay. We had enough income that I could stay home to raise Crew. I could work a couple of "at home" side jobs for some extra money when I needed to. I loved the cute little house we had remodeled and were living in. Things seemed to be working out really well—everything, that is, except for our relationship with Crew.

Over the next nine years, Brett and I struggled with Crew. He became more and more challenging, and he spent more time out of control than in control. The older he got, the worse it seemed to be, and that aggravated me. I could not control him, and that also scared me. I started searching for ways that I could help him, and I spent years and years and tens of thousands of dollars doing just that—all to no avail.

Ultimately, I found the solution when I started to look for the value in our day-to-day challenges with Crew. As much work as I had done, I was still holding on to some of the guilt, particularly when he and I would have a bad day. I was not seeing the greater picture or the purpose behind the pain. I was always looking to end the pain: my pain, Crew's pain, Brett's pain. But instead, what I really needed to do was appreciate the pain, appreciate the entire situation. It took me nine years to realize that appreciation was the missing piece. I was so busy trying to fix, heal, deny, or control the situation that I wasn't looking at any of it as a gift.

With the support of both my physical and nonphysical teachers, I began to see—and, more importantly, to appreciate—the greatest lesson of my life, the one being taught to me by my son, the greatest teacher in my life. I had been missing the whole point for so long that it kept my son and me stuck in a never-ending pattern. The gift was in the value of our experience. Hmm. Think about that for a minute. This is the biggie. The gift, the lesson, the message, the answer is in finding the value of the experience. Once you find the value, you step away from the pain, judgment, anger, and fear. Once you step away from the negatives, you allow yourself to be grateful, appreciative, and whole.

To get there, on a daily basis, I had to start looking at myself. I had to start seeing through the mirror my son was holding for me. I had to take the focus off of what he needed and see clearly what it was that I needed. For both of us to heal, I needed to be appreciative. I needed to own the experience, understand the purpose, and find the value. Then, and only then, would I be able to love fully, wholly, and unconditionally.

This was not easy. Those years were some of the most difficult of my life—of all of our lives. Finding the value was a challenge. My son came here to teach me, and he took his job *very* seriously. He was an intense teacher. He had me in tears a lot of the time. He mirrored so much pain to me that it was indeed hard to look at. How did I even begin to find the value? But it is as simple as it sounds. The way I found the value was to look at what I had learned. Ultimately, through all of the ups and downs over the past two decades, I learned to love and accept myself. I learned to forgive myself for the past, and I learned what unconditional love was. My son had mirrored my pain for me all of those years so that I could move through it all into that place of self-love. And in that, I had finally found the value in all of our experiences—and for that, I am forever grateful.

Nearly twenty-two years ago, when I thought my life was

ending, who could have known that this little Spirit who had entered my body would teach me how to heal my heart? He did, I did, and *everything happens for a reason.*

∾

I have worked these steps for many, many years and can now fully appreciate the "bigger picture" that I was not aware of while I was in the experience. Applying these steps has not only healed my heart, but it has given me tools that I can now share with you. I hope as you work through each of the nine steps that your journey is lighter and more joyful. When the student is ready, the teacher appears, in whatever form is needed. As a teacher, I have discovered that I teach what I need to learn the most. Self-love, acceptance, and forgiveness were absent from my life, and I have learned to embrace each one wholeheartedly. Love is an endless journey that I look forward to moment by moment through grace, ease, and the divine guidance of the Archangels. It is my hope that these steps move you toward appreciation of the amazing person you are and the phenomenal life you can create today!

Please enjoy this poem from my son Crew, written for me on Mother's Day 2009. This shows you how, when you get into appreciation, appreciation is returned tenfold.

One in a Million Mom

One in a million
That's what they all say
Every single year
On Mother's Day

How many go deep
And say so much more
To let their mom know
That they are adored

You stuck up for me
When I didn't know
Put me in a car
Said honey let's go

We moved to AZ
Found the right man
Became a family
And here I still stand

I think about the past
What you took me from
I resent nothing you did
You were just being a mom

What makes me smile
Gives me glee
Is the fact
That you did it all for me

Not many people
Would go through the thought
Without a next move
Possibly getting caught

Many struggles
Nobody knows
But I understand
I watched you grow

Funny to think
That you watch your son
He grows up
You think you're done

I watched you
All the same
Grow and mature
Come to fame

I saw your tears
Heartache and fun
I saw my mom
And I will never be done

I will stay your son
Your little baby man
No matter how old I get
I will do what I can

I appreciate your help
On levels so high
You may never understand
As much as you try

But in the end
I think you know
I look to you
To help me grow

Forever I see
You and me
We'll stick together
You're my queen BEE.

—Crew Dylan Johnston, 2009

Working with the Nine-Step Archangel Process

Angels have no philosophy, but love.
—Terri Guillemets

The Nine-Step Process to Healing Addiction

Step 1: Awareness

For many of you, the step of awareness, when dealing with any type of addiction, will coincide with your realization that you have "hit rock bottom." The actual event, trigger, length of time, or motivation will be uniquely your own, but the end result will be the realization that you are out of control and that your particular addiction, whatever it may be, is actually what is in control of you.

Step 2: Looking Within

When dealing with an addiction, looking within can be very difficult, because not looking within is the reason you became addicted in the first place. Our drug or "behavior pattern" of choice has been present in our lives to serve as a distraction from the feelings and emotions often discovered when we stop the addiction. This step requires tremendous courage, the ability to ask for help, and the willingness to receive assistance from the Archangels and Spirit Guides to help you face your fears, move past your judgments, and be open to the guidance within.

Step 3: Choice

No matter what your motivation for change is, you must arrive at a place in your life where making the choice to change is less painful than living in the addiction. Making this choice moves you toward an unfamiliar yet healthier life experience.

Step 4: Commitment

Addiction causes people to maintain the illusion of control. This step often requires the willingness to admit you need help so that you can take the next step. You will need some form of support, and asking the Archangels to surround you and guide you is one *big* step toward making a commitment. You may also need the support of professionals to assist you in your healing.

Step 5: Responsibility

This is a pivotal step in breaking the cycle of addiction, because it forces you to drop the blame-and-victim role that has been masking the internal pain you've been feeling. Once you take responsibility for your life, and all that it has become, by taking back your power from the addiction, you can then harness that power within to create the life you truly desire.

Step 6: Action

As with many twelve-step programs, the action of "one day at a time" is the way to begin your journey toward healing your heart. It is important to be present each and every day with your feelings and emotions, while invoking the healing energies of the Archangels to assist you. Follow the guidance you receive as you move forward to the next step that can support you in your goal.

Step 7: Releasing and Replenishing

As new behavior patterns strengthen and grow, you'll continue to discover layers of emotions as you move toward complete wholeness. Finding a tool that helps you feel safe and supported is key to processing these emotions and reinforcing your sense of well-being.

Step 8: Maintenance

Addictive patterns can be incredibly powerful! You must remember to support yourself with the energy of Archangel Michael, as well as other physical beings who understand the energy it takes to maintain new behaviors, boundaries, and a higher vibration.

Step 9: Appreciation

By understanding the value of *all* the experiences that you've had so far, you can heal the pain at the core of your addiction by entering a state of appreciation. Appreciation opens the door to forgiveness, which eventually makes you feel whole again.

Working with the Steps: A Client's Experience in Applying the Nine Steps to Addiction

I was a drug addict spiraling out of control. My body was failing, my marriage was failing, and I was failing my children. I hit rock bottom and found the strength within these steps, and the energy of the Archangels, to heal myself from the inside out.

Step 1: Awareness

After countless bladder infections, sinusitis, being forty pounds underweight, and a multitude of destructive behaviors, I challenged myself to abstain from using methamphetamine for twenty-four hours. After having used this drug recreationally for a year and daily for four years, I wanted to prove to myself that I was a different kind of addict. I was an addict who could control my drug use—I could stop anytime I wanted. Within a couple of hours, though, I quickly became aware of how difficult this would be and how strong my urge was to "use" when emotions surfaced, and I didn't know what to do with them.

This was my first awareness experience. I had the awareness of "feelings" and "emotions" that began to surface that I just couldn't handle. My feelings erupted even more when I hugged my son that same day. For the first time in a long time, I could "feel" my son's heart connect with mine, and I could feel the warmth of him in my arms as we embraced. And in that moment, I stood still . . . and I "felt," instead of denying my emotions through the manic pace that using "meth" had left me in. I realized that I wasn't any different from any other addict. Soon after this awareness, I began to journal. Writing gave me a safe place to express myself as I hit what I refer to now as my rock bottom. Everyone's rock bottom is different, and no one could convince me that I was out of control until I was ready to see it for myself. It took me a year to begin to move into a place of recovery.

Step 2: Looking Within

This was my most difficult step. I was terrified of my feelings and emotions. For years, I had kept myself numb with meth, and now I no longer wanted to hide in the world that I had created. There were days, however, when I wondered if the path to wholeness and healing was really worth it. I was feeling so much pain and was uncertain of my future. I knew how to live a life masking feelings of abandonment, frustration, sadness, and self-judgment, but I didn't know how to deal with years of pain that I had bottled up inside. The more I journaled, the deeper I went into these feelings—my journal felt like the only safe place that I could go to express myself. Guilt and shame filled me as I began to look at the environment I was raising my children in. The one person I hadn't wanted to become—my father—was who I had become. The only difference between us was our drug of choice, and that was extremely painful to look at.

Step 3: Choice

I did not recognize my own value or worth. I spent years looking outside myself for the energy that I needed to carry me through whatever issue I was having at the time. When I realized this, I made a choice. I made a phone call to a recovery hotline to see if someone could help me, so I would not have to feel this pain anymore. My kids became my reason for wanting to heal. My kids were my life, and I wanted to feel their love in the same way I had when I'd embraced my son the day I tried not to use meth for one day. This gave me a reason to get clean, it gave me a reason to change, and it gave me the energy within to make the choice I did.

Step 4: Commitment

After I made the choice to get clean, I was overwhelmed with all of the chaos I had created, and I had no idea how I was going to get through this all by myself. I was afraid to let *anyone* know how out of control I felt. My marriage was falling apart and I was depressed; my kids started wondering what was wrong, since I cried at the drop of a hat, and my entire emotional well-being felt unstable. I had tried to quit cold turkey, and, after three months, I realized that I needed professional help. I had to let go of an old belief: I was taught when I was a child that asking for help was a sign of weakness. Somewhere, something inside me knew that I needed to open up and ask for help. This was my first invitation to the Archangels to help guide me to where I needed to go to pull my life back together again; thus my commitment to my children and ultimately myself began.

Step 5: Responsibility

I had blamed my dad and his alcoholism for many years, so learning to let go of my victim mentality was difficult, to say the least. Owning that I had done this to myself was painful, but somehow I began to slowly share my feelings with my closest family and friends. For the most part, I received love and support, except from my dad. Within moments of feeling his rejection, I realized that it didn't matter what he or anyone else thought. This was my journey, and I was sharing from my heart, regardless of the outcome. After thirty-plus years, I finally took responsibility for the life I had created. The more I realized that my life was my own creation, the more my motivation for wanting to get well shifted from my kids to myself. For the first time, I wanted to pull my life together for me.

Step 6: Action

The action step was exhausting for me. I found a psychotherapist whom I felt comfortable with to help me release the layers of feelings and emotions that had been buried deep inside. This was a time of self-discovery. I found the strength and courage inside to connect with other people who were living the type of life I wanted to create for myself. When the physical cravings overwhelmed me, I would go outside and feel the space all around me. I would bask in the feelings of freedom, strength, and peace and find comfort in the petals of a rose. I would stare endlessly at their formation while I focused on my breath, allowing my body to relax so I could let the uneasiness pass.

I not only worked on the emotional and physical aspects of my addiction, but I started to use affirmations. Each time I drove by the community college that I wanted to attend, I would affirm to myself: "Someday I am going to go there!" My therapist gave me a wooden "TUIT" coin as a going-away present. As she placed the coin in my hand, she smiled and said, "Now you have a 'round Tuit,' it's time to go do it." A round TUIT is a reminder to get "around to it," to take action and move forward and take the next step. With this new sense of comfort and strength, I took action and enrolled in "Women in Transition," a class at the local community college. All it took was one action step and then the rest of the way became clear as I kept moving to places of love and support. Through this process, I was guided to Sunny and her healing center, Sunlight Alliance LLC. It was in this place of safety and love that I was able to find my Spirit and learn to love myself from the place I was.

Step 7: Releasing and Replenishing

This process really took me by surprise. By allowing myself the time and space to feel, without knowing all the hows and whys, I have found the process of releasing to be a tremendous help. A year before I quit using meth, I was journaling every day, and I wrote many letters to people with whom I needed to share feelings and emotions. Some of the letters I shared with others, the rest I kept to myself. I was amazed at the emotional release I felt as I moved through the pages of my journals. Journaling has become an effective tool to release what's in my heart, mind, body, and spirit. Journaling is a safe place for me to own my power and fill myself with the love and compassion I need once I've emptied the painful places.

Step 8: Maintenance

Learning to set healthy boundaries, surrounding myself with like-minded people, making a commitment to attend classes, events, or lectures that support my own personal power, and asking for help are all ways in which I have learned to show up for myself. At times, I may stray from what I know to be in my best interest, but one thing I have learned is that I can never lose the knowledge I have gained. Since I have become clean, there are still times when I want to hide from the world, but I call on the energy of the Angels to help me reengage with my community of support. Having the strength and courage to see that is priceless!

Step 9: Appreciation

Appreciation for me is standing in the space of a great accomplishment and welcoming the gratitude and abundance of the experience. Every day is full of value and lessons. Some days are more difficult than others, and it is during the difficult ones that I need to make a conscious effort to embrace my awareness of appreciation. The road that I have traveled from an addict out of control to an open, embracing, and loving human being has been supported by the energy and love of the Archangels. Even though I was not always aware of their presence, the mere fact that when I asked for help, invoked their energy, and allowed them to help on my behalf, they were there—for that, I am grateful.

The Nine-Step Process to Healing an Unfulfilled Career

Step 1: Awareness

Challenges with your career can involve a specific job, location, co-worker, etc. In any scenario, the first step in dealing with the issue will involve acknowledging and identifying that something is not working for you any longer.

Step 2: Looking Within

Because our career is often a way we define ourselves and our self-worth in society, it is important that we look within ourselves to really get honest about what the root cause of our discontent or discomfort might be.

Step 3: Choice

As you gain clarity from within, you will gather information that will help you to weigh your options. Many times, fear of change can immobilize you. Asking for guidance from the Angels can give you the faith necessary to make a choice and trust that you are being guided for your highest good.

Step 4: Commitment

Once your choice is made, you can manifest it into reality much more quickly by fully applying your passion and enthusiasm in that direction.

Step 5: Responsibility

Recognizing your responsibility in attracting your desired outcome is critical. To bring the positive energy into the career area, you must look at your part in creating the experience you are now living. Once you have owned that responsibility, you can move away from blame, frustration, and resistance, and move toward what you truly wish to create.

Step 6: Action

Believe in yourself and move forward with inspired action. Listen to your guidance as you prepare yourself to step into a new vibration in regard to your career. This may manifest as a new job or just shifting the energy in the environment you are already in.

Step 7: Releasing and Replenishing

Identify any thoughts or feelings that might be holding you back from experiencing true success. Journaling is a great way to release the fears and allow yourself to see clearly what you are holding inside. Invoke Archangel Raphael to help you let go of thoughts that no longer serve you. Replenish yourself by imagining how you will feel when you are doing what you love. Write a list of the qualities you want to experience or the way you want to feel in your career environment and then affirm them out loud.

Step 8: Maintenance

Each and every work environment causes you to deal with a variety of people, many with different goals and priorities from your own. It is especially important to establish a consistent method of protecting your energy while doing your job. Recognize the need for setting and maintaining healthy boundaries, become an observer, and practice detachment where necessary so that you can continue to keep your vibration and enthusiasm at a higher level.

Step 9: Appreciation

Recognize that every experience that comes to you in your career has the potential to provide you with growth and expansion. Seeing the value, the growth, and development in every experience you have had will make you much happier, healthier, and positive within yourself—and in any workplace.

Working with the Steps: A Client's Experience in Applying the Nine Steps to Career

At age forty-five, I left a high-stress, upper management, top-salaried position for a chance to create a vocation that today has become my life's work. This career change was one of the biggest challenges of my life, and I have found this nine-step process to be an integral part of my journey.

Step 1: Awareness

In 1999, my dad died at the age of sixty. It was early, unexpected, devastating—and it changed my life forever. I was working in a prestigious job as a project manager in an information technology department, and even though I had feelings of discontent and emptiness, I ignored them. I was caught up in financial security and the ways in which the business world fed my ego. However, during my dad's brief illness, I struggled with my inability to relieve his pain; it was during this time that I became aware that my heart was empty and that there had to be more to life. The visions of his discomfort haunted me and gave me the insight that I needed to make a change. I could only identify bits and pieces of what I was searching for, but I knew that I had a desire, a strong desire, to help humanity. Looking back, I did not invoke a specific Archangel; however, I am now aware that the energy of Archangel Chamuel was very present as I questioned my life purpose and career.

Step 2: Looking Within

After my father died, I took some time off of work and finally had the space and freedom to look within. I was guided to two important books: *The Power of Now*, by Eckhart Tolle, and *Ask and It Is Given*, by Jerry and Esther Hicks. After reading these books, my perception of what resources I had, even within me, changed. I also did a lot of journaling at this time. Initially, writing served as an outlet for my grief. But I began to discover that journaling was a method to connect to and receive messages from the angelic realm and my inner voice. When I began to listen, the urgings for something greater still persisted. Even though I was not ready to leave my established job, I continued to look within.

Step 3: Choice

As the urgings from my inner self grew louder and louder, I could no longer ignore them. I became ever more weary of my high-profile job, and I knew that, sooner or later, I would have to make a choice. Over time, my feelings of discontent began to shift my previous resistance to change. It became more uncomfortable to stay where I was than to move forward. Something from within was helping me to believe in a better end result, even though I didn't know where I was going. So, I quit my job and walked away from my comfortable prison.

I found that I was feeling more trust that I would be guided to the next step. I believe this was the energy of the angelic realm that was all around me. I initially began a business as a part-time landscape photographer. This was a safe way for me to follow my urgings to feed my Spirit. I loved to take pictures, and I loved to be outdoors, so the two fit perfectly. As I spent time in nature, I was able to create more space to listen within, and I began to discern the qualities I was looking for in my future "life's work." This was also the first time that I had made a choice to do things that put *me* first. Over time, these baby steps led to a move across the country to attend classes at the Boulder College of Massage Therapy. I had indeed made another choice.

Step 4: Commitment

I discovered many times during this journey that when I made a decision and committed fully, the pieces suddenly clicked into place, and the "hows" magically materialized. I didn't need to do any more than commit. By going "all in" and lining up my vibration behind my choices, the next set of doors opened. My early transition steps into photography had reignited my own enthusiasm and passion, and I finally rediscovered how to allow myself the freedom to explore something I loved to do without first "figuring it all out." I made the commitment to listen to my inner voice and wisdom. I committed to living my life from my heart rather than my ego. Once I had this committed energy to work with, it made dealing with obstacles easier, while keeping my vision on the prize and payoff at the end. This commitment served me well, as a year later, I graduated from massage school with top honors.

Step 5: Responsibility

During this entire transition time, I knew that I was accountable for the life I was creating. I was right where I was because of my choices. I knew this, but I had to work hard to keep the faith in my own power to create the things I was striving for. As my journey continued to unfold, I struggled with feelings of defeat when opportunities did not present themselves as I "thought" they should. But because

I believed that my thoughts and beliefs were responsible for what I manifested in my life, at the very least I knew I needed to find a way to stay neutral in my emotions when my passion and enthusiasm waned. So instead of worrying endlessly or obsessing over Craigslist for my next place of employment, I returned to nature and played with the dog or pulled weeds from my garden.

I took responsibility for moving funky energy out, so I would not sabotage future opportunities that were on their way. And when opportunities did come along, even the less desirable assignments in the early days of my massage career, I realized their hidden benefits in the opportunities to refine techniques, improve business skills, or gain marketing ideas. These experiences continued to reinforce for me the importance of responsibility and how my "stinking thinking" could be my own worst enemy.

Step 6: Action

If you want to find your dream job, then you have to put yourself out there and believe in yourself. There were times when I was more positive and optimistic about the job market, and that's when my greatest action steps took place. I would send out résumés, make contacts, review potential work spaces, and take extra classes—all in an effort to keep moving. I understood the value of staying neutral with my emotions as I waited for my dream job. I would land small massage jobs here and there that would teach me new skills or help me continue to define my dream job. As I got more experience under my belt, I began to trust in myself and my abilities. My confidence kept growing, and I was finally given the perfect opportunity to create the massage practice that I wanted. The action steps that I took (and sometimes did not take) paid off, for in the end, I was being led to what I had wanted all along.

Step 7: Releasing and Replenishing

I found this step challenging. I am my own worst critic and at times struggle with the high (sometimes unrealistic) standards I have set for myself. I needed to find ways to relax and release my own judgment and expectations. It was important for me to move through any self-defeating behaviors when opportunities were slow to materialize. I went back to my old standby tool of journaling to help release my anxiety. I spent more time in nature, putting my hands in the dirt. These acts rejuvenated my Spirit, and I felt replenished. I know now the peaceful energy of Archangel Uriel was present with me. His energy was in nature and in the dirt of Mother Earth, and it helped me find peace, clarity, and insight.

Today, I have built a successful practice, and the nature of my work requires me to use my tools and Uriel's energy to release anything that I might have absorbed during the day working with my clients. I also call in Archangel Michael to help me protect my energy and Archangel Raphael to restore me from within. These Archangels have become key components in my own wellness plan.

Step 8: Maintenance

I am now working as a full-time massage therapist. It is a profession that feeds my Spirit. Every day, I instinctively call upon the Archangels to help me be a clear channel for healing and to protect and support me in the work I do. As

I mentioned earlier, Archangel Michael is my go-to guy. Every morning before I start work, I envision his protective blue bubble surrounding me as I work with my own energy and the energy of each of my clients. I ask him for strength and guidance as I do my massages. And I call in Archangel Raphael to direct healing energy to my clients—to help them to release all that no longer serves them and fill every cell of their body with Divine love and acceptance. I ask that their own Inner Physician lead them down their path to complete health and wellness.

My morning mantra or affirmation has become: "I am Open and Receptive to All that is Good." This key phrase that I learned from Sunny years ago is the one thing that has been the common denominator as my dreams for a more meaningful career materialized. This one affirmation helps me feel the connection to my inner guidance and is protection from negativity (both the internal and external varieties).

Step 9: Appreciation

Eleven years have passed, and through the twists and turns of my journey, I now know that losing my dad was the trigger that opened up my awareness and began my relationship with my Angels, guides, and my inner self. Every day, I feel more and more appreciative for each experience. My father's untimely death still pulls at me, and the images of the pain he suffered continue to haunt me, but I am moving toward more appreciation as Archangel Chamuel teaches me about unconditional love.

I needed a catalyst for change, and his death shook up my world enough to start the ball rolling. Had that not happened,

I would still probably be a project manager making lots of money and living an unfulfilled life. Instead, my talents as a massage therapist are in high demand at the local healing center. I practice from my heart, and I am grateful for the chance to be of service, doing what I love to do, and sharing it in a space of peace and healing every day.

The Nine-Step Process to Healing Relationships

Step 1: Awareness

For many, the step of awareness when dealing with relationships will coincide with a breakdown or failure within a relationship. Any relationship or interaction with another person can serve as a mirror for you. By seeing an issue in another person, it illuminates something that you may not have had an awareness of within yourself. Through your relationship, awareness can be brought to the surface.

Step 2: Looking Within

Often it is the repetition of patterns in your relationships that allows you to recognize the need to examine any thoughts, perceptions, or emotions that may be playing a role in these interactions. This step can be a struggle, as it is often easier to blame someone else rather than uncover the painful pieces of yourself that you have tried to avoid.

Step 3: Choice

In any relationship, you always have choices. Some require more strength and courage, but you are never alone or without options. Calling in Archangel Michael to help you push through the difficult options can help you actively participate in your choices, rather than doing nothing—which is a choice in and of itself.

Step 4: Commitment

Because a loving relationship begins with your ability to love yourself, committing to discover all the ways in which you can better appreciate and value yourself is always the first priority. You must be willing to love yourself enough.

Step 5: Responsibility

Especially in challenging relationships, the tendency is to find blame with everyone around you. No matter what the circumstances may be in your relationship, you must arrive at a place where you can own the fact that you have created these experiences, that you have attracted them into your life, and that you can change them.

Step 6: Action

To have a healthy, loving relationship, you must be willing to act as if you love yourself without conditions. In this step, when you "act as if," you actually begin to experience that love for yourself, which can then expand out toward others. Archangel Chamuel is especially helpful in bringing the energy of unconditional love into your experience.

Step 7: Releasing and Replenishing

In many cases, relationships suffer from the baggage that both individuals bring to the partnership. An important area to focus on is identifying and releasing the old memories and emotions that are sabotaging your ability to love yourself and others. Asking for help in letting go is key, as is replacing the negative energy with positive affirmations, visualizations, and actions.

Step 8: Maintenance

As you do the work to achieve self-love and attract that similar energy into your relationship, it becomes essential that you maintain healthy boundaries with everyone you interact with. Maintaining your own power, your energy, is an absolute must in sustaining the positive feelings that you are now experiencing.

Step 9: Appreciation

Every interaction provides you with an opportunity to learn more about yourself, as well as the person who serves as your mirror. When you move into a place of appreciation, you will experience your relationships—all of them, as challenging as they may be—as amazing gifts in your life. Once you see the value in your relationships, you will automatically see and feel the vibration of love and happiness within you, and that love and acceptance can then be shared with others.

Working with the Steps: A Client's Experience in Applying the Nine Steps to Relationships

My husband of fourteen years picked up and left me one day with no explanation. I was devastated! I had no spirit, self-esteem, or self-worth, and I was so depressed I just wanted to die. These steps helped me move through that experience and learn to love myself again.

Step 1: Awareness

The life that I was familiar with and loved ended abruptly, and I told my friends that if anyone cut me open, they would see a black hole the size of the Grand Canyon. I felt depressed for months and was so low, there was no place else left to go. Somewhere, deep down inside, I knew I had to do something, because this kind of life was not for me.

So, I made an appointment with a counselor. Many sessions left me sobbing and in so much pain that I could barely take a breath. I kept saying to myself over and over: "There has to be something wrong with me." My counselor countered with: "There is nothing wrong with you. This is about him—not you." And I'd come back even stronger with: "But he left *me!* You don't understand."

In the midst of this crisis, I also lost my job and had far more free time on my hands than I cared for. I'd sit outside in my yard and sob for hours. One day I cried so hard, I slumped over and either passed out or fell asleep from exhaustion. This went on for months; then one day, while I was driving in the center lane of the 101, I found myself thinking, "I just wish I could die and end this pain forever!" Just as I finished that thought, a truck in front of me ran over something that flew up in the air in a huge backward circular motion and came right at me. I watched in slow motion as half a steel-belted radial tire hit my windshield and shattered it. The truck kept going, and somehow I managed to exit the freeway and drive home amongst all the broken glass and frayed nerves. I called the insurance company and they sent someone out right away to fix my windshield. The repairman could not believe the damage, and he told me that he only saw this amount when dealing with head-on collisions. He said to me, "You know, you're very lucky! A piece of tire that big could have taken your head off."

That was my moment of awareness! I remember processing his words and looking up to the heavens as I mentally said to myself, "Okay, I got it, Angels! I got it!" His remark had brought me the awareness of my current state of being and that shook me to my core. After that experience, I never uttered to myself or anyone else again that I wanted to die.

Step 2: Looking Within

I began with Al-Anon meetings, since my soon-to-be ex-husband and I were both adult children of alcoholics. I went for while, but something stirred inside, and I knew I needed to do something else. I tried Unity church and befriended a woman on my second visit. She mentioned that she had just signed up for a class on Archangels with a woman named Sunny and that it was going to be held at the local community college. I was intrigued and decided to go. I absorbed everything said in the class about who the seven Archangels were and what they did.

Since I am a highly visual person, I needed something to look at to help me find clarity. I purchased a deck of Angel cards and began to work with them daily. Seeing the faces of the Angels and reading what the cards said helped me to identify the work I needed to do. I made an appointment with Sunny and signed up for her six-week Angels 101 class. My process of looking within began.

Step 3: Choice

I was tired of being miserable, and I made the choice to get better. I began by calling in the blue light of Archangel Michael each morning. There were days when it hurt so bad, all I could do was cry. I struggled with believing that the Archangels would help me. I would say to myself, "Who am I for an Angel to help me?" But I made the choice to continue working with Archangel Michael despite my negative self-talk.

Step 4: Commitment

I committed to working with the Archangels and my cards each day. I started using affirmations. When I began journaling, I could only express anger. Sometimes I wrote so hard that I'd tear through several pages of paper. I bought a huge brown envelope and wrote in big black marker: "When I die, give this to X." I wanted my ex-husband to know the pain he had caused.

I'd flip between being a "new" person and an angry person. It was a struggle to not blame myself and feel guilty. How could I let this happen? As time progressed, I found a job. I committed to getting up thirty minutes earlier each morning, so I could do my affirmations and work with my cards. I visualized myself surrounded by the blue light of Archangel Michael and invoked the pink light of unconditional love of Archangel Chamuel. I wore blue and pink clothes to help me keep the vibration of each Archangel throughout my day.

Step 5: Responsibility

It took me a while, but I finally realized that I had created this misery by giving and not receiving. Looking at this was difficult, so in taking responsibility for my actions, I decided to start receiving from myself. I purchased a new journal and agreed to only fill it up with positive thoughts. I took a long, hard look at everything that happened and only wrote things that supported my Spirit. I wanted to feel whole again, and even though I had no idea how that would happen, I knew that with the help of God and the Angels, I could!

Step 6: Action

Beside taking classes, using Archangel cards, saying positive affirmations, and journaling, I began to separate myself from everyone and everything that brought me down. I started making new friends whose vibrations matched those of where I wanted to be. Even though it was challenging for me to stay at a higher vibration, I was able to do this for short bursts of time.

Little by little, I maintained a higher vibration and positive thought process for longer periods of time. One of my classmates actually said they thought I "looked" different—I was smiling, and that was something I hadn't done much. Slowly these actions and the Archangels helped me adjust my attitude, behavior, and thoughts. I started believing that maybe, just maybe, I was worthy enough for the Angels to spend time with and care about me.

Step 7: Releasing and Replenishing

The more I released, the more I realized that I did not know how to replenish. Replenishing was a foreign concept to me, and I had no idea how to do it. I went to the store one day and saw a cat about six months old wandering in the parking lot. She looked exactly like my last cat, Buster, whom I'd had to put down a short time before. Someone picked up the cat and took it inside the pet store. I followed them in because I'd decided that I wanted the cat if no one else was going to take it home. They scanned for a microchip and did not find one. That was all I needed to hear, and I took the cat home that day.

Because I did not know how to love and replenish myself, I knew that I needed something else. The Archangels were guiding me to this cat, which I named Cookie, to help me feel the connection of love that I had been missing. So for the first time in a long time, I began to replenish my Spirit with the love from my cat.

Step 8: Maintenance

I love stones, especially the ones that reflect the colors of the Archangels. I meditate each morning with the stone that I feel I need that day. I also choose to wear clothes that match the color of the angelic energy that I would like to invoke. I bring the stone, its color, and the energy of the Archangels into my awareness and quietly sit as I wait to hear messages. Sometimes I get messages, sometimes I don't. I sense the stone's importance to becoming one with my Spirit and just sit quietly with it.

I am also a person who honors nature—the plants, animals, sun, moon, and stars. For me, part of maintaining is honoring Mother Earth, and, through that, I honor who I am. I enjoy sitting in nature with my cats and just "being." When I think of that, I smile, and by honoring my Spirit daily, I am able to hold on to who I am becoming.

Step 9: Appreciation

I appreciate the angelic realm because they were working overtime on my behalf for a long time, even when I was unaware of it. They surrounded me with love, supported me when I could not support or love myself, and loved me through all of it. They guided me to places, people, and events that helped me become whole. They stirred the "who" of who I *am* for me to become who I am today. For that, I am forever grateful.

Another Client's Experience in Applying the Nine Steps to Relationships

More than anything, I wanted to be in a relationship with a man. I thought this kind of love would fill me up and make me happy. In past relationships, I have ignored my intuition and endangered my son and myself because I was in search of the impossible. These nine steps have helped me realize that before I can be in a healthy, loving relationship, I need to love myself first.

Step 1: Awareness

I wanted to experience a healthy, loving relationship with a man. My desire to find someone who would marry me and fill me up even took precedent over my gut feelings that told me this individual was not healthy for me or my son. My intuition told me, but I chose to ignore it for the sake of "being in a relationship." As time went on, this man threatened to kill me, blow up my car, and ruin everything I had. Despite all of that, when it was time to end the relationship, I was crushed. He was supposed to be "The One" who was going to love me through thick and thin. I hit rock bottom. I felt like a failure. I couldn't believe that I had put myself and my son in such danger. For the first time, I became aware. I became aware that I was looking for someone to love me, so that I would not have to do it myself. I became aware that I couldn't see my own value and self-worth, because I was blinded by the fear that I was unlovable. With that awareness, I began to heal.

Step 2: Looking Within

Failed relationships had become the norm, and I finally concluded that the problem was "me." I started the painful process of looking within. I hated myself, but secretly had hoped that someone in this world would find me lovable, even if I didn't love myself. I began to recognize that the level of vibration I was working from was exactly what I kept attracting back to me. I didn't feel worthy of such a loving relationship, nor did I believe that someone could love me despite my flaws; therefore, I did not find myself in a relationship that was healthy and loving. By looking within, I was able to realize that a loving relationship began with me.

Step 3: Choice

How could I begin to love myself? Feeling like a failure was getting really old, so I thought I would try something new. I made a choice and began taking classes with Sunny at her healing center, Sunlight Alliance. She was instrumental in helping me learn ways in which I could love myself. At first, loving myself seemed like a foreign concept. I felt a lot of resistance to even considering it as a possibility. But I soon decided: "What did I have to lose?" So I gave it a shot by making another choice: to try. Sunny introduced me to Archangel Michael and encouraged me to invoke his energy for protection each time I looked deeper and deeper within. I asked him to surround me with his blue light and to protect me from any negative thoughts I was having about giving up. His strength was instrumental in helping me make choices that were based on loving myself.

Step 4: Commitment

I made a commitment to myself to learn "who I was" and to start appreciating what I had to offer. If I could find appreciation in me, then perhaps others would see it as well. I struggled with this, since no one had loved me before, but my Spirit knew that this was the next step and wouldn't let me quit. I didn't know how to start. This was uncharted water for me. However, I did know that Archangel Jophiel was the Angel who could help me see the beauty within myself and show me how to manifest what I desired. So I invoked the yellow light of Archangel Jophiel to surround me daily. I asked him to help me believe in myself and to manifest the life I truly desired. With Jophiel's loving energy, I was able to set some goals that I was willing to commit to.

Step 5: Responsibility

Taking responsibility for my failed relationships was hard for me. It was much easier to blame others and convince myself that "they" were missing out on what a great person I was. But in my heart, I knew this wasn't true, and as I sat with the idea of responsibility, I had to look within and accept my part in all of this. I had searched my entire life for the one thing I was never able to find, and that was self-love. So now

I had to take responsibility for my actions and beliefs around the notion that I could be loved. This was a very pivotal moment in my process.

Step 6: Action

With the realization that I was responsible for feeling loved, I knew I needed some help in taking the steps necessary to shift into that belief pattern. Sunny had taught me about Archangel Chamuel, the Angel of unconditional love and adoration. She told me to start saying positive, loving affirmations in the mirror every day, even though I did not believe them at first. I started by faking it. I repeated these affirmations over and over again, because that is what I was supposed to do. It got easier as time went on, and I was eventually able to look into my own eyes as I repeated these loving words to myself.

I felt like my heart was opening for the first time. This intrigued me, and I wanted to feel more of it, so I continued with this every day. Archangel Chamuel played a huge role in my process. I invoked his pink light and asked him to surround me each morning to assist me in accepting unconditional love for myself. If I noticed negative thoughts creeping in, I immediately changed them to something positive. I not only invoked Chamuel but also Raphael. Archangel Raphael is the Angel of healing. I asked him to help me heal the deep, deep hurts I had in my heart. Each morning, I envisioned his green energy surrounding me, and somehow I just felt better. The process of integrating these new actions into my daily routine was an incredible time in my life.

Step 7: Releasing and Replenishing

Releasing past experiences and failed relationships was extremely emotional for me. Forgiving myself was very difficult. I started journaling at this time, and this helped me allow the buried emotions inside me to surface. This was a really scary time. What if someone read my journal and found out about all the pain and heartache I carried? Putting my emotions and pain on paper made them real. I was surprised at what came out and my heart ached as I poured my soul out. As I wrote each word, I could feel each emotion as I let it go.

Part of releasing is replenishing; and to do that, I had to forgive myself. I invoked the energy of Archangel Zadkiel to help me with forgiveness. Sunny suggested that burning the letters would be a way to release the feelings and emotions. So, when I was done writing, I did just that. I invoked the purple light of Archangel Zadkiel and envisioned him surrounding me as I watched my words burn away. This process of releasing felt so empowering. The heaviness that I had felt for so long finally lifted, and I felt lighter. As I released, I replenished with the loving, healing energy of the Archangels. Every day, I would envision them filling me up and making me whole again.

Step 8: Maintenance

For me, maintenance begins with boundaries. I have found a new self-love for myself, and it is important to surround myself with friends and family that vibrate at this same level. Through this process, I can now see that it is my responsibility to love myself enough to only allow into my space those who lift me up. If I want to have a healthy, loving relationship, then I must have integrity with myself. I remind myself every day that I deserve to be happy and successful. Having people around me who believe the same thing and can mirror it back to me is of the utmost importance. I now choose relationships that are healthy and happy for me, instead of choosing from a lack of self-worth.

Step 9: Appreciation

Appreciation is being able to stand in a place of understanding the experience gained with each relationship. Learning the value of each experience allows you to move through it. Archangel Uriel played an essential part in appreciation. I invoked the red light of Uriel to assist me in understanding the value of each failed relationship and to note what lesson I took away from each experience. I began to see how each choice I made helped to define what I truly desired and to know that I was worthy of a healthy relationship. Each experience helped me evolve into the person I am today. I am in the process of creating the life I desire, and my studies with Sunny have helped me get there. Her teachings about the power of the Archangels have been instrumental in healing my heart and in loving myself. What a wonderful blessing Sunny and the Archangels are.

The Nine-Step Process to Health

Step 1: Awareness

For many, the step of awareness when dealing with health will coincide with a breakdown or failure of the body.

Oftentimes physical pain is your first sign that something is out of alignment. The pain can be chronic or acute, and you can choose to acknowledge it or not. Awareness can also come through routine physicals, cholesterol checks, or blood pressure checks. You might not feel anything, but a random test reveals that something is not right.

Step 2: Looking Within

When you receive a diagnosis or an indicator, it is important to look within and evaluate your emotional health. Often, repressed emotions and feelings surface through disease or ill health. Our bodies are wonderful guidance systems, letting us know when things are working or not working. It is in this step that you must be willing to look within and see what emotions might be causing your body to indicate something other than wellness.

Step 3: Choice

When it comes to your physical health, you are the creator of your reality. In any moment, you can choose wellness or you can choose sickness. Sometimes, the fear of a diagnosis prevents you from going to the doctor, or a busy schedule leaves you without any time for a routine physical. Invoking the Archangels to help you make healthy decisions is important in this step, for often your well-being comes last unless you are forced to pay attention.

Step 4: Commitment

Wellness begins with you. No one else is responsible for what goes into your body. It is important to make a commitment from a place of love and not fear. Making a commitment to change your diet, start an exercise program, or change the vibration of your thoughts is a positive step toward health. Call on Archangel Michael to help you maintain your commitment, because a healthy body leads to a happy heart.

Step 5: Responsibility

Oftentimes when a diagnosis is received, the tendency is to give your power away to the doctor who is treating you. Sometimes it is easier to take a pill or have a surgery than it is to heal the issue from the root emotional cause. There are situations in which it is important to work in tandem with the medical community, but also remember you have a natural healer within you that knows the way to wellness. Sometimes it is easier to blame than take responsibility for your health. I encourage you to work with Archangel Raphael, as he can support you in listening to your own inner guidance.

Step 6: Action

To have a healthy body, you must be willing to take action. Action can come in the form of a healthy diet, a Reiki session, a medical test, a counselor, a massage, or a new workout routine. The point is, you must be willing to love yourself back to wellness and to take action that supports that. Archangel Chamuel is especially helpful in bringing the energy of unconditional love as you discern what action steps are appropriate for you.

Step 7: Releasing and Replenishing

In most cases, disease shows up in your body due to unresolved emotions and feelings. Your body is your greatest indicator that something is out of alignment, and releasing all negative emotion is the key to your well-being. Often emotions have been repressed for quite some time, and it is important to ask for help as you begin to release. Replenishing yourself is *very* important as well. If you release old energy but don't replace it with new loving energy, your body will return to what it knows. Listen to your body, and fill it up in whatever loving way the Angels guide you to.

Step 8: Maintenance

As you work to release emotions and feelings, it is important to protect your energy, uphold your boundaries, and maintain a positive vibration. If you don't do this, then you risk breaking down your physical, emotional, mental, and spiritual resources. Your day-to-day well-being is dependent on your emotional state, and Archangel Michael can help you witness rather than absorb any negative energies around you.

Step 9: Appreciation

Many people who have had serious illnesses talk of appreciation and value. Often when you are faced with challenges that are life threatening, you start to value your life and make changes that shift your entire perception of who you are. Physical challenges get your attention, and, through each experience, you have an opportunity to discover the gifts. Once you see the value of your health, you will automatically see the vibration of love and well-being that exists within you.

Working with the Steps: A Client's Experience in Applying the Nine Steps to Health

My life came to a complete halt when I literally could not stand up. This incident caused me to pay attention to my physical body and to ultimately make the choice to stop eating foods that made me sick. I wasn't prepared for the onslaught of emotions and feelings that occurred once I removed gluten from my diet. These steps and the energy of the Archangels helped me maintain my commitment to my health.

Step 1: Awareness

I woke up one morning, and as I tried to get out of bed, I tumbled to the floor because I could not gain my balance. I tried to focus on an object in the room, and all it did was spin around. I felt as if I were on a merry-go-round; I wasn't, so I knew something was medically wrong. I was scared, so I called the doctor and got in to see her right away. She was certain that it was vertigo, but just to be sure, she ran a complete blood series on me to rule out other issues. When the results came back, several of the values were out of normal range. My iron and ferritin levels were so low that the doctor was concerned I was bleeding internally and wanted to rule out cancer. She advised me to schedule a colonoscopy right away so they could see what was happening inside my body. All I did was go to the doctor's office to find out what was making me dizzy; imagine my surprise when she gave me reading materials about a colonoscopy procedure. In the span of an hour, I became very aware that something was going on with my body.

Step 2: Looking Within

I went home that evening and sat with the doctor's concerns and my blood test results. I got quiet, closed my eyes, touched my heart, and just listened. I listened for an answer to my question: "Does this ring true for me?" I didn't feel like a victim; I didn't ask "Why me? How did I get this?" I just listened. And what I heard from within and from the angelic realm was that I didn't have cancer, but there were some things going on that needed further evaluation. Part of looking within for me was acknowledging that I was unaware of any physical issues that might be happening. It was difficult to admit that I was more tuned in to what was happening from a spiritual perspective than I was from a physical perspective. My body was trying to talk to me, and I needed to listen—so it got my attention in the only way it knew how. It stopped me in my tracks.

Step 3: Choice

I made a choice. I decided to go ahead with the colonoscopy to rule out any other health concerns, as I was certain that they were not going to find any cancer. I had the procedure less than a week later, and, as I suspected, they did not find any cancer or polyps. They concluded that the low levels of iron and ferritin were due to malabsorption by my digestive tract, which typically indicates a gluten intolerance. I was relieved and quite happy to hear it was "just" a gluten intolerance.

Over the next several days, I read everything I could find on gluten. Gluten is a protein that is found in wheat, Khorasan wheat (brand name KAMUT), spelt, barley, rye, malts, flavorings, and stabilizing or thickening agents. I discovered that gluten was in just about everything. All I could think of was no more pizza, cake, ice cream, bread, pancakes, French toast, Subway sandwiches, or cereal, just to name a few. My gosh, I *loved* cereal. It was supposed to be good for you, fortified, and loaded with vitamins—and full of gluten. My carefree response to "just a gluten intolerance" was quickly fading. How was I going to eat food that was gluten free? Where would I find it? How would I afford it? What was I going to eat when everyone else was eating all the "normal" foods? I had to have a "come to Jesus" moment with myself and make a choice. I could either continue to eat the way I had been or go gluten free. I made the choice to go gluten free.

Step 4: Commitment

Once I'd made the choice to go gluten free, my commitment to my health and well-being was challenged every day. Whether it was at work, restaurants, weekend parties, or family get-togethers, there was always food that contained gluten. I even had to deal with family and friends who insisted that a little piece of Mom's home-baked pie would not kill me. This only added to my own internal struggle to give up foods I loved. That was the first time I found myself saying "Why me?" and that was usually when the cookie tray was going around. So this step was a challenge for me and, to this day, continues to be a challenge.

When I reach for something that contains gluten, I try to pause and go within and seek the assistance of Archangel Michael. I ask myself what purpose this food will fill. Most of the time, the support of Archangel Michael's energy relieves the need to have it. But sometimes, all I want is a chocolate chip cookie. When those moments happen, I allow myself to eat the cookie, as long as I take a digestive enzyme to aid in the breakdown of the gluten. What I found to be of most value in invoking Archangel Michael is his ability to help me protect my energy and stay centered in my vision of well-being. He helps me hold on to my commitment when the Italian pizza cravings come up.

Step 5: Responsibility

I quickly became responsible and accountable for my life when I realized that the only way I could ensure that I was eating gluten-free food was to prepare it myself. I got tired of going out and eating foods that I thought were gluten free but turned out not to be. Usually within a couple of hours of eating, I was in the bathroom being sick. I did fairly well in restaurants, because there was always an option of a meat and vegetables, but outside that, it was difficult.

I also had to take responsibility for my health. When I made the choice to go gluten free, I knew this would be a major life change. I had created this situation with the foods I'd eaten, and now I needed to re-create a healthy body. I knew no one could do it but me.

Step 6: Action

The action step for me was really quite simple. I quit eating gluten. I threw out all the foods in the cupboards that contained gluten and cleared out the refrigerator and freezer so that I could have a fresh start. I did more research on the Internet and discovered that there were other terms used on manufacturing labels that essentially meant gluten, so I made a list of them and printed it. I also began taking iron supplements and vitamin D to help restore my body to a healthy state.

In the beginning, cutting out gluten was difficult. I discovered that I was an emotional eater, and the foods that normally pacified my moods were no longer acceptable. I felt irritated, short with people, and cranky as I removed these "lifelong friends" from my diet; I had to take steps to deal with the emotions that surfaced once my diet dramatically changed. I called on Archangel Raphael to help me with the cravings and to support me as I moved through the emotions.

Step 7: Releasing and Replenishing

Releasing is an ongoing process for me as I continue to become aware of how my "choice of food" is directly related to the emotions I am feeling. I always used to say, "There's nothing in this world that can't be fixed with a chocolate chip cookie." Well, not anymore—a chocolate chip cookie is not going to fix my health.

I invoke Archangel Raphael to support me as I become aware and comfortable with feelings and emotions. I'd much rather spend my days in the spiritual ethers, disconnected from my physical body, because I am safe there—it's my home. Releasing is difficult, as I've always been an emotional "stuffer." I'd never learned how to express anything other than happiness. Happiness I can deal with. Good times I can deal with, but fear, pain, and anger—not so much.

I continue to look for ways to release. I am a singer/song-writer and have found great comfort in the lyrics of a song I am writing or the rhythm of the beat. Music and my guitar have become a way for me to release and replenish, and I am grateful for that as I continue on this journey. So for me, this step is ongoing.

Step 8: Maintenance

I have surrounded myself with friends and family who are supportive of my journey. Now when I go home for Christmas, my sister whips up a batch of gluten-free chocolate chip cookies, and I love her for that. When I attend parties, my friends always make sure there is something gluten free for me to eat. My dear friend Sunny helps me look at emotions and feelings every day, and I am blessed to have a partner who chooses to walk this gluten-free path with me. Food is an extremely powerful soother for me, and to maintain my commitment to health, I invoke Archangel Michael to help me protect my energy. I realized through this whole process that I absorb others' feelings and emotions in a snap, and often it is then that I want the comfort of food the most. Archangel Michael helps me keep my energy field clear and clean so I can make healthy decisions about what I will eat and not eat.

Step 9: Appreciation

I found it interesting that I created a situation in which I could no longer use my "comfort foods" to mask my emotions, because they were making me physically sick. In looking at the value of this experience, I know that I physically feel better when I do not eat gluten. I am learning how to *feel* my feelings, instead of stuffing them down. Although it can be uncomfortable, I know it is the best choice for my health.

I am appreciative of the vertigo episode, because the extreme dizziness got my attention. When I couldn't stand without falling over, I had to come back into my physical body and be present in it. I had to come back into my emotional body and open up to it. Feeling good is something I appreciate every day, and I continue to work with the Archangels as I allow myself to experience wellness—body, mind, and soul.

Guided Angel Meditations

Angels are spirits, but it is not because they are spirits
that they are angels. They become angels when they are
sent. For the name angel refers to their office, not their
nature. You ask the name of this nature, it is spirit; you
ask its office, it is that of an Angel, which is a messenger.

—St. Augustine

Connecting with your Guardian Angel and/or the Archangels provides an opportunity to gain healing, awareness,
and protection for not only yourself but the people around
you! I use the following exercises as part of my daily medita-
tive practice. By invoking the Angels in this way, I offer an
intention of love and healing for all humanity. You may want
to ask a friend to read these aloud to you or read and reflect
on your own. If you'd like to download these guided medita-
tions via your computer, please go to our interactive website
www.invokingthearchangels.com.

Invocation of the Archangels:
A Guided Meditation

Begin by invoking Michael, the Archangel of protection. He stands to your right. You call him in by saying (in your mind or out loud): "I now invoke the mighty and powerful blue light of Archangel Michael to surround me and protect me. I ask for strength, courage, direction, and protection from any negativity, seen or unseen. Please use your electric-blue sword to release any doubts, fear, or worries. Thank you . . . and so it is."

Now, listen quietly within to receive any special message Michael has for you.

Next invoke Uriel to stand to your left side. "I now invoke the mighty and powerful Archangel Uriel to stand on my left-hand side. Please release all my anger, worries, and fears. Please surround me with your wisdom, peace, and joy. Please help me to serve others with an open heart so that I may learn to receive and give with generosity, appreciation, and kindness. Thank you . . . and so it is."

Now, feeling Uriel's presence, become aware of any guidance or wisdom that he may have for you.

When you're feeling ready to invoke Archangel Raphael, begin by imagining a beautiful emerald-green energy completely enveloping you. This is the light of Archangel Raphael and his healing vibration. "I now invoke the mighty and powerful Archangel Raphael to stand before me. Please surround me and fill me with health, well-being, and wholeness. Help me to heal any wounds—physical, mental, emotional, and spiritual—from the past or present. Please heal and restore every aspect of my being. Thank you . . . and so it is."

Feel the healing energy flowing through you as you feel a personal message from Raphael in your physical body.

Visualize the white light of Gabriel coming down from the heavens and entering your body through your crown. Feel Gabriel's energy of communication and clarity. "I now invoke the mighty and powerful Archangel Gabriel to stand behind me. Please bring me insights and awareness so that I may always speak truth. Remove all my doubts and fears, and allow me to express myself in a loving way through mind, body, and spirit. Thank you . . . and so it is."

Take a moment to relax, listen, and open your heart to a message that Gabriel is sending you.

Focus now on your heart center and the gentleness of Archangel Chamuel. "I now invoke the mighty and powerful pink light of Archangel Chamuel to expand the love I have in my heart. Please help me to find unconditional love and compassion for myself and others. Allow me to love and accept myself exactly as I am and witness that love returning to me. Thank you . . . and so it is."

Now, feeling Chamuel's presence in your heart space, become aware of any guidance or wisdom that he may have for you.

Now you see a beautiful golden-yellow energy encircling you, and you know that Archangel Jophiel is surrounding you. "I now invoke the powerful Archangel Jophiel to surround me in the golden light of beauty and manifestation. I ask that you guide me and inspire me to see the beauty life has to offer, to affirm and witness the positive in each and

every experience. Allow me to be a teacher of positive manifestation and creativity. Thank you . . . and so it is."

Take a deep breath and know within your mind the message that Jophiel is sending you.

Finally, you find yourself supported by the violet ray of
forgiveness and mercy, and you know that Archangel Zadkiel is present. "I now invoke the mighty Archangel Zadkiel
to help me surrender and release any judgment, criticism, or
neglect from myself or others. I ask for all my pain and negativity to be released and replaced with peace, joy, tolerance,
and love. I ask for forgiveness on all levels. Thank you . . .
and so it is."

Feel the energy of forgiveness and joy flowing through
you as you feel a personal message from Archangel Zadkiel.

Now that you have invoked the Archangels, allow yourself to bathe in their unconditional love, divine perfection,
and peace. As human beings, we often tend to visualize the
Archangels as beautiful winged beings. It makes no difference how you perceive the Archangels. They will come to
you in the way you believe them to be. So your experience
of them is perfect for you! All you have to do is remember to
take a few moments and invite them into your life. You will
experience miracles when you do this. I have!

Guardian Angel Meditation: A Guided Meditation

Let's begin by closing your eyes and relaxing your body.
Take a deep cleansing breath, in through your nose and out
through your mouth. Another deep breath, in through your

nose and out through your mouth. As you continue taking deep breaths, allow your physical body to melt into the chair or the floor beneath you. As you begin to relax your body, let any tension drift away. Let any thoughts, worries, or concerns drift right out of your mind as you continue to breathe in, and out.

Visualize a rich, vibrant, colorful room. This room is like nothing you've seen before. Notice what color the outside of the room is. When you feel ready, open the door to the room. As you enter, you begin to feel an amazing sense of calm and quiet. Look around and feel the energy of the room. You'll notice a door off to the left. Move toward the door and open it. As you walk through the door, you'll be greeted by a beautiful spiral staircase that leads downstairs. Begin walking down the staircase, one step at a time, until you reach the bottom.

When you get to the bottom, you'll notice three beautiful doors. The door to your right is electric blue, the door in the center is emerald green, and the door to your left is a rosy pink. As you observe the three doors, you'll find that you are drawn to one of them, and you begin walking toward that door. As you walk, you can feel an overwhelming sense of peace and love.

If you walked to the electric-blue door, then you can feel a sensation of protection, guidance, and courage as Archangel Michael stands at your side. If you chose the emerald-green door, you feel the powerful healing energy of Archangel Raphael as he moves to your side to work with you. And if you chose the rosy-pink door, then Archangel Chamuel's love and compassion embrace you as he appears. Visualize your Archangel standing in front of you. Your Archangel reaches out and takes your hand. You can feel the warmth of his touch, and you begin to feel completely relaxed and at ease as you know you are safe in his arms.

As you relax even deeper, you notice that you and your Archangel have drifted to another place. That place is your most exquisite place on earth. Notice where you are. Is there sand at your feet? Are you standing in a flower-filled garden? Are you frolicking in the ocean? Take a minute and feel the peace that fills your heart, the joy, harmony, and love that you are experiencing. Notice if there are any scents. Can you hear the sound of birds or water or perhaps even leaves falling? Take a moment to experience this place that your Archangel has taken you. Feel it . . . embrace it.

Your Archangel gently takes your hand again and begins to lead you toward a gorgeous bright light. He turns to you and says, "It's time to meet your Guardian Angel." Appearing right before you is your resplendent, loving, gentle Guardian Angel. You can feel the unconditional loving energy of your Guardian Angel as you meet him for the very first time. Get to know your Guardian Angel. What is his/her name? What messages might he have for you? Take the next few minutes to listen to the guidance that your Guardian Angel has for you.

Finally, share with your Guardian Angel how very glad you are to have had this time together. It is now time to leave this special place. Thank your Guardian Angel and Michael—or Raphael or Chamuel—as you turn to leave. As you walk back, you'll find yourself in the rich, vibrant, colorful room where you began. When you feel ready, you can open your eyes and be present again in your physical space. Namasté.

SECTION 7

A Few Clients'
Angelic Experiences

Angels are all around us, all the time,
in the very air we breathe.
—Eileen Elias Freeman

We are experiencing the angelic realm in many ways that
often go sight unseen. Or, even worse, unnoticed. We pass
them off as coincidences or strange or odd events, but the
truth is that Angels exist in our lives. They exist in all of our
lives, if we will only look with an open heart and an open
mind. In the next few pages, clients and students of mine
will share their own personal Archangel experiences. I have
not rewritten their stories, except in a couple of instances for
clarity. This is how they expressed their experiences with the
angelic realm after asking to be guided. Many of the stories
are written directly to me, so when someone writes, "then
you said . . ." or "you had us do . . . ," I am the "you." I share
these stories with you to give you a broader sense of all of
the ways that your Angels and the Archangels can manifest

in your life. From the subtle to the downright "in your face" variety, our Angels are always working with us, to share with us the energy of love in all of its many forms.

Archangel Chamuel

My husband died five years ago. The loss and grief were unimaginable. I'd lost my best friend. I had to find a way through it, and that need, that determination, set me on a path of magical discovery for which I will be forever grateful. At the two-and-a-half-year point, I felt compelled to write a book about all that I was experiencing with the hope that, by sharing my experience, I could help others find their path through loss. My journey has continued, and I feel another book brewing. And this conference will definitely be a part of it!

I first attended the Celebrate Your Life conference in 2007. Wow! It was just where I needed to be. I went again in 2008, but skipped 2009. This year I went, looking forward to hearing new speakers, like you, and to meet my Reiki "grandmother," Ann Albers. I feel so blessed to have been there, and it was definitely where I was supposed to be. The Angels' guidance was everywhere, and it felt wonderful.

In your workshop on Saturday, I missed the first exercise—Hand on Heart—having gone to the ladies' room. When I returned, I took my seat in the back of the room, where I tend to sit at these workshops. I thought the exercise would be over, but it had just begun. Everyone had a partner already, so I sat in the midst of all that loving energy, closed my eyes, and just enjoyed the feel of it all.

It was nearing the end of the workshop, and we were all

hugging the people around us. When I returned to my seat, there was someone right next to me who hadn't been there before. I thought I'd seen him come up the aisle from the front of the room. I wondered why he was moving now, near the end, and why he chose that seat. There were lots of other places to sit! The chairs were in disarray from the earlier exercise, and these two isolated seats were right next to each other without even an inch between them.

In my mind, I clearly heard the words, "You're in trouble." But there was no sting attached to them, just the hint of a smile. I knew there was going to be one last exercise, and I knew that this person would be my partner. There was no way out. Though I hadn't even looked at his face yet, I'd "known" it was a man. We were so close, I could feel him. Well, everything happens for a reason, I told myself.

Now you may be thinking: So what, it's a man. But in my life I am rarely around men. In the last five years, I have only had Dad hugs and son-in-law hugs. Being an elementary school teacher, I work mostly with women. The groups I am involved with outside work are also made up of women. In recent months, I'd found I couldn't even relate to romantic movies with men and women caring about each other. I knew what it was like to have a loving relationship with a man, so why, suddenly, couldn't I relate to this idea?

At this point, you asked people to find a partner. The man and I looked at each other and agreed to be partners. (He told me, by the way, that this was the third workshop he'd been to; he'd walked out of two others that morning.) We sat with our knees touching, then got closer still. By this time, he was holding my hands, and we were looking into each other's eyes. You hadn't yet said what we would be doing. But all was okay, I told myself. I sensed that he was a gentle and genuine person.

And then you said, "You will touch your partner's face." Oh my! My partner asked me if I was willing and I said I was. (Mostly, I knew there was no way out, and that, reluctant or not, I was where I was supposed to be.) We had already been looking into each other's eyes for quite a while when he began to touch my face. I couldn't stop the tears from flowing, and I fought to keep myself from trembling. (And even now as I write, here come the tears.) Then I touched his face, trying so hard to stop my hands from shaking. And the tears continued to flow—so many tears.

When the Archangel Chamuel exercise ended, the workshop was over. The only words I could get out were, "Thank you. You gave me a great gift." As I left the room, I tried to look nonchalant and not give away my real feelings of wanting to run away before I broke apart. I headed for the closest ladies' room, found a stall, shut the door, and sobbed my heart out.

I had recently suspected that I had grown quite a suit of armor around myself. In Ann Albers's workshop the day before, she had talked about if you hold everything in too long, it's like the little boy with his finger in the dike—powee!—it will all explode one day. And that's exactly what it felt like now.

I had not been touched so lovingly in over five years. I'd taught myself to think that I didn't miss it, didn't need it, and lately, worst of all, that it wasn't even possible. But anything is possible. I, of all people, should know that. In the last five years, I have learned to feel and sense the wonderful universe around us in ways I never thought possible. I am full of gratitude for it all, and the path continues to open up before me. Thank you, Sunny, for creating a space for such happenings to occur. They are priceless gifts.

—*Allyn*

Archangel Michael

I was devastated when my dog of nine blissful years, Leo, passed away unexpectedly. I was completely disconnected from my Spirit and was really angry and upset. (I guess that's what happens when you are in shock.) I had a very hard time understanding and making sense of it all. Mostly I was frustrated with my son, because he was the one who had accidentally let him out of our yard. At the suggestion of a dear friend, I spent some time in my bathtub (that's my quiet meditation place) and tried to make sense of it all.

Just the week before, I had held my grandfather's hand as he transitioned to the other side. I felt some sadness, of course, but I was at peace knowing that he was at peace. With my dog, however, I was hysterical! So, while sobbing uncontrollably in the bath, I had an extremely calming experience with Archangel Michael that I will *never* forget. What I recall very distinctly and quite vividly was a feeling of a really "large" presence behind/above me. There was almost a lull, like being in a place where I wasn't quite awake yet not quite asleep. There was so much love and peace, it's difficult to put into words. I "heard" a firm but loving voice telling me that Leo was okay and that I didn't need him anymore. I think it really only lasted a few seconds, but it felt like a much longer time span, and all I can really remember was feeling a sense of complete relaxation and peace. I also believe that through this experience, I was able to heal a lot of the anger I had toward my son.

Grief is a strange thing; it doesn't wear a watch, so of course I have experienced more sadness and such, but knowing that Michael showed up when I was in complete despair, really helps me to feel connected to Leo now. I have since had countless experiences of finding random feathers that are left as a reminder that Leo is not far from us, and I know to my very core that he is not alone, nor am I.

—*Marci*

Archangel Uriel

Sunny, your class had such an impact on me yesterday that I decided to take your Archangel exercise to heart. I had picked "red" for Tuesday (Archangel Uriel), so I put on my brightest red shirt and tie for work that day. I also realized I had a sculpture of Archangel Uriel that friends had given me years ago; I had put it into my room right before the Celebrate Your Life weekend.

As I was driving to work, slowly singing the name U-ri-el several times, I saw a shadow figure on the side of the building where I work, on the window near my office. On the way to taking my daughter, Paislee, to school fifteen minutes later, I caught a glimpse of the sign of the business nearby: Angels in Waiting. Finally, I noticed a picture [of a red Angel] that Paislee had created for me a few years ago right above the phone I use every day.

Wow!! It is amazing how Uriel showed up for me all day. I

felt his energy throughout the day, no matter the challenges that were before me. Thanks so much from the bottom of my heart. I want you to know that your workshop was more powerful and changed me on a deeper level than the rest of the Celebrate Your Life weekend combined.

Thanks, Sunny, for being so open, so honest, so real with who you are—for it has allowed me to see more clearly who I really am. With heartfelt love and gratitude,

—Jim and Archangel Uriel ;-)

Archangels Michael and Raphael

My uncle has been struggling with addiction, chronic pain, and psychological/financial/marital issues for more than twenty years. He and his wife had two children together. Due to his diseases throughout the years, there was constant turmoil, abuse, and a toxic environment that made it a very sad and inappropriate setting for a family to thrive in. Several "interventions" from my parents throughout the years only led to the same vicious cycle, and he would fall back into the same toxic routine. Today, my father and his four siblings, as well as my mother, all came together and visited him at his house for a final offer of help.

While they were at his home, I stayed behind and called on the Angels, particularly Archangels Michael and Raphael, for strength and healing for my uncle. I visualized him being surrounded by an entourage of Angels; I asked them to give him the strength to admit that he needed help and to agree to go to Maryland with his sister where he could live a structured lifestyle, follow a healthy diet, help out around her property, volunteer to help those in need, and, of course, stay clean. I opened my heart and let loving energy flow from it directly to my uncle while continuously calling on the Angels.

Twenty minutes later, they came back with him; he had finally agreed to seek the help he so desperately needed. I was immediately filled with gratitude and indescribable joy, and I ran straight to my uncle and gave him a long hug. I could feel the presence of the Angels surrounding us. It was an experience I will hold close to my heart for the rest of my life.

—*Lindsey*

Archangel Michael

When I was beginning my spiritual journey in 2000, I was learning to talk with the Angels and journal our conversations. My mom was very sick in the hospital, and my connection to the Angels and God was getting stronger each day. One night when I went to bed, I asked Archangel Michael what he wanted me to know. What message did he have for me? I soon became very calm and relaxed and saw, in my mind's eye, my mom in the hospital. Each of her grandkids went to visit her. I saw as each one arrived, and what they were wearing as they went in to see her. I then saw a beautiful field and a hill of wildflowers. I felt so at peace. I knew this was a sign that my mom was going to be okay. I heard Archangel Michael tell me not to worry.

All of a sudden, everything was very, very bright, and I took off flying—actually flying! I was astral traveling with Archangel Michael. We flew through the bright, bright blue sky, and the clouds were amazingly bright white. I felt myself gliding through the skies. It was the most amazing feeling. I did not want to stop. Everything was so crisp, clear, bright, and beautiful. The colors were magnificent. The next thing I knew, I'd woken up, and it was the next day. I went to visit my mom in the hospital. Soon her grandkids arrived—in the order that I had seen the night before in my mind's eye! Everything was exactly as I had seen it. Her granddaughter, Lindsay, and my niece drew on the chalk board in the waiting room a picture of a hill and field of wildflowers! I knew then that Archangel Michael had given me a wonderful and awesome message. I thanked him at that time. I will never forget the wonderful message and astral travel I had with Archangel Michael.

—*Jan*

Guardian Angel

In December 2009, my wife and I went to a friend's house to deliver some comfort food [because her mom was] not doing well. She had stage IV cancer and was living on pain medication. When we arrived, we stood outside the room where her mother was resting and talked to the dad; once in a while, we glanced into the room. The woman lying in the bed could not have weighed more than ninety pounds. She used to be full of life, healthy, and strong. The next time I glanced over, I saw a young woman lying next to her in the bed; she was very beautiful and looked at me, smiled, and continued smiling and laughing while talking to [the mom]. When our friend went into the room to administer the pain medication by eyedropper, the young woman watched very closely. We left a few minutes later; while driving home, I told my wife that it was really sad being there, but it was also so nice to see who I assumed was a granddaughter lying next to her. My wife said no one was in the room but the mom, and no one was ever lying next to her. Within about an hour, we were informed of her passing.

We asked her daughter the next day if her mother had been the only one in the room that night, and she confirmed that she was. My description of the Angel fit the description of a dream the mother's other daughter had had.

—Tom

Appendix

I saw the angel in marble and carved him
until I set him free.

—Michelangelo

Invocations for the Archangels

These invocations can be read aloud, said silently in prayer, or meditated upon. Use your own intuition to guide you to the best way for you. You can also try one way, have an experience with it, and if it feels in alignment, stay with it. If it does not resonate with you, try a new invocation or another way of invoking it, through written word, vision, or intention. Ultimately, your Spirit knows what is best for you, so listen to the answers and guidance within.

Archangel Michael

Archangel Michael before me.
Archangel Michael behind me.
Archangel Michael above me.
Archangel Michael all around me.
Archangel Michael, thank you for surrounding me . . . and so it is.

∾

I invoke the blue light of Archangel Michael to surround me and protect me from any negative energy or
entities. And so it is.
(Feel the sapphire-blue light in front of you and see
yourself step into this light.)

∾

Archangel Michael, please come to me now and help
me to maintain my own energy with grace and ease;
please surround me in your light.

∾

I now invoke the blue light of Archangel Michael to surround and protect each and every one of us. I ask him to
bring us courage and strength and to protect us from any
negativity, seen or unseen. I ask that the brilliant blue
energy of protection be placed over us all, so that only
that which is of the highest good can surround us.

Archangel Gabriel

I now invoke Archangel Gabriel to stand beside us
in his pure white ray. I ask that he surround us in his
white energy of purity and peace. I ask that he help
each of us to communicate with intention that which
we desire—with our words, thoughts, and feelings of
light and love.

Archangel Uriel

I now invoke the energy of Archangel Uriel to stand in
front of us and fill us with the ray of wisdom and peace.
Help us to soothe all conflict in our life and replace it
with knowledge and understanding of what our true
purpose is on this planet. We ask that his energy help us
to learn and teach that which we need in each moment.

Archangel Raphael

I now invoke the green light of Archangel Raphael to stand behind us. I ask that he pour healing and abundance into us all. I ask that he help us to allow the healing to be received, and that he guide us through our own physical, mental, emotional, and spiritual healing each and every day.

Archangel Chamuel

I now invoke the light of Archangel Chamuel and its pink ray to expand the unconditional love in our hearts. Please help us to find compassion and unconditional love for ourselves and for everyone we have ever harmed, knowingly and unknowingly. We ask that our hearts be opened to receiving and giving that unconditional love.

Archangel Jophiel

I now invoke Archangel Jophiel to pour the golden light of wisdom and illumination onto us. We ask that we be able to see the true beauty within ourselves and each situation. We ask that the awareness of true beauty lie within our hearts and help us to connect to the oneness that we truly are.

Archangel Zadkiel

I now invoke the light of Archangel Zadkiel and its violet ray of mercy, joy, and transmutation to surround us in violet flame. We ask for all our negativity to be released and dissolved and replaced with joy. We ask that the energy of true forgiveness blow through us and heal the areas in our lives where forgiveness is needed, beginning with the forgiveness of ourselves.

"Blue Bubble" Visualization

Each morning, before stepping out of bed, do the following exercise. Lie or sit up in bed, quiet yourself and your mind, and visualize a sapphire-blue bubble completely surrounding you. Imagine yourself completely embraced by this beautiful brilliant energy, and as you do, know that you are completely surrounded and protected from negative energies. You do this not so much to protect yourself from another's negative energies, although it will, but more so to strengthen and maintain your own personal energy field so that it continually revitalizes you throughout the day.

Prayers

White Light Prayer

I call on the Archangels, Ascended Masters, Spirit Guides, and helpers to surround me in white light and to guide me and protect me. I ask that you work through me to clear any anger, fear, judgment, or guilt. I ask that my Spirit be an open and clear channel to provide the highest good for all concerned. Thank you for surrounding me. I am filled with the Spirit of love and light, always and in all ways . . . and so it is.

Prayer of Healing for Mother Earth

Dear Spirit,

I ask that you help me open to your love, wisdom, and healing energy. I ask for a connection to the Master Teachers: Christ, Buddha, Mother Mary, Kuan Yin, and others who are sending love and healing to Mother Earth at this time. I ask for the loving and healing energies of the Angels of Light to move through me into the Earth and to the people that live on her, to be utilized in whatever ways are highest and best for them. I ask for the energies of strength, love, support, and healing to be sent to all inhabitants of the planet. I, _____ [fill in your name], stand for the healing, recovery, and restoration of the balance of the land, the infrastructure, and the people in highest Divine Right Order. Thank you, Spirit, for this opportunity to be of service.

American Indian Prayer for Peace

Let us know peace. For as long as the moon shall rise, for as long as the rivers shall flow,

For as long as the sun shall shine, for as long as the grass shall grow, let us know peace.

Guardian Angel Prayer

Guardian Angel from heaven so bright,
Watching beside me to lead me aright,
Fold thy wings 'round me, and guard me with love,
Softly sing songs to me of heaven above.
Amen

Angelic Positive Affirmations

I am loved, unconditionally

I am open to my Guardian Angels

I am protected and guided by my Angels

I trust that my guide will attract only miracles in my life

I am open to my healing Angels

I am thankful for my life and my Angel of perception

I am now surrounded by Angels

The Angels shine the love of the Universe upon me
and through me

I accept love from the Angels

I call upon the Archangels to help and guide me

My inner voice and feelings are guidance from the
Angels

I know that the Angels love me and are guiding me
right now

I accept the Angels' love

My Angels and I enjoy new opportunities to give
service to the world

The Angel of Inspiration guides me to do anything I
truly desire

I am divinely guided by the Angel of Happiness

I am divinely guided by the Angels toward optimal
health

I am peace

I am divinely guided by the Angel of Patience

I trust my loved ones will be protected by the Angels

I believe in the Universe's messengers, the Angels

Angel Sayings

My Angels love me unconditionally; I feel calm and relaxed as I release all my fears and worries to them.

I have faith in Angels and my future.

If life becomes too much to bear, remember your Angel is always there.

We hold the key to our own happiness, but Angels guide us to the right doors.

Angels don't worry about you. They believe in you.

While we are sleeping, Angels have conversations with our souls.

Angels are often silent, but they are listening to every thought that stirs our souls.

Angels help you pick up the necessary pieces of your life and leave the others behind.

If you seek an Angel with an open heart, you shall always find one.

A gathering of Angels can enlighten the whole world.

Angels occupy the loveliest corners of our thoughts.

Angels encourage us by guiding us onto a path that will lead to happiness and hope.

Give of yourself as the Angels do, and wonderful things will come to you.

A house call from an Angel can heal a broken heart.

Angels may not come when you call them, but they'll always be there when you need them.

An Angel doesn't have to be physical to touch you.

When hearts listen, Angels sing.

He who has fed a stranger may have fed an Angel.

Angels are the guardians of hope and wonder, the keepers of magic and dreams.

Our Angels watch over us and communicate with us in unseen ways every day.

Suggested Reading

Listed here are some of the books that I have found very supportive and helpful throughout my journey. You may find they serve you well, too.

Beattie, Melody. *Codependent No More: How to Stop Controlling Others and Start Caring for Yourself.* Center City, MN: Hazelden Publishing, 1987.

Braden, Gregg. *The Divine Matrix: Bridging Time, Space, Miracles, and Belief.* Carlsbad, CA: Hay House, 2007.

Byrne, Rhonda. *The Secret.* New York: Atria Books; Hillsboro, OR: Beyond Words, 2006.

Chapman, Gary. *The Five Love Languages: The Secret to Love That Lasts,* 2nd edition. Chicago, IL: Northfield Publishing, 1995.

Choquette, Sonia. *The Psychic Pathway: A Workbook for Reawakening the Voice of Your Soul.* New York: Carol Trade Paperbacks, 1995.

Course in Miracles, A: Combined Volume. Glen Ellen, CA: Foundation for Inner Peace, 1992.

Gibran, Khalil. *The Prophet.* New York: Alfred A. Knopf, 1973.

Grabhorn, Lynn. *Excuse Me, Your Life Is Waiting: The Astonishing Power of Feelings.* Charlottesville, VA: Hampton Roads Publishing, 2000.

Hay, Louise. *You Can Heal Your Life.* Santa Monica, CA: Hay House, 1987.

Hicks, Esther, and Jerry Hicks. *Ask and It Is Given: Learning to Manifest Your Desires.* Santa Monica, CA: Hay House, 2005.

Jampolsky, Gerald. *Teach Only Love: The Twelve Principles of Attitudinal Healing*. Hillsboro, OR: Beyond Words, 2000.

Leaf, Caroline. *Who Switched Off My Brain? Controlling Toxic Thoughts and Emotions*. Nashville, TN: Thomas Nelson Publishers, 2009.

Pradervand, Pierre. *The Gentle Art of Blessing: Lessons for Living Your Spirituality in Everyday Life*. Fawnskin, CA: Personhood Press, 2003.

Redfield, James. *The Celestine Prophecy: An Adventure*. New York: Warner Books, 1993.

Ruiz, Don Miguel. *The Four Agreements: A Practical Guide to Personal Freedom*. San Rafael, CA: Amber Allen Publishing, 1997.

Stein, Diane. *Essential Reiki: A Complete Guide to the Ancient Healing Art*. Freedom, CA: Crossing Press, 1995.

Tipping, Colin. *Radical Forgiveness: A Revolutionary Five-Stage Process*. Boulder, CO: Sounds True Publishing, 2009.

Tolle, Eckhart. *The Power of Now: A Guide to Spiritual Enlightenment*. Novato, CA: New World Library, 1999.

Virtue, Doreen, and Lynnette Brown. *Angel Numbers: The Angels Explain the Meaning of 111, 444, and Other Numbers in Your Life*. Carlsbad, CA: Hay House, 2005.

Reader's Notes

About the Author

SUNNY DAWN JOHNSTON is an inspirational speaker, a compassionate spiritual teacher, an internationally acclaimed psychic medium, and an author. She has been featured on numerous local and national television and radio shows, including *Coast to Coast* with George Noory. In 2003, Sunny founded Sunlight Alliance LLC, a spiritual teaching and healing center in Glendale, Arizona. She also volunteers her time as a psychic investigator for the international organization *FIND ME*. This is a nonprofit organization of psychic, investigative, and canine search-and-rescue volunteers, working together to provide leads to law enforcement and families of missing persons and homicide victims.

Sunny lives in the sunshine of the Arizona desert with her husband Brett, sons, Crew and Arizona, and their two dogs, Pelé and Xena. To learn more about Sunny's work, see videos, and read articles, please go to www.sunnydawnjohnston.com.

To join in a fun and interactive Facebook page, please check out www.facebook.com/SunnyDawnJohnstonFanPage.

Sunny has created an interactive website for your enjoyment and participation with other readers of *Invoking the Archangels*. This interactive website offers support, fun, community, and great nuggets of wisdom. To have an interactive experience with others reading this book, please visit www.invokingthearchangels.com.